Turkey Calls
and
Calling

Turkey Calls and Calling

Guide to Improving Your Turkey-Talking Skills

STEVE HICKOFF

STACKPOLE
BOOKS

Published by
STACKPOLE BOOKS
5067 Ritter Road
Mechanicsburg, PA 17055
www.stackpolebooks.com

Printed in China

10 9 8 7 6 5 4 3 2 1

First edition

Photography by the author, unless otherwise noted
Cover photos by National Wild Turkey Federation
Cover design by Wendy A. Reynolds

Library of Congress Cataloging-in-Publication Data
Hickoff, Steve, 1958 –
    Turkey calls and calling: guide to improving your turkey-talking skills /
Steve Hickoff. — 1st ed.
        p. cm.
    Includes index.
    ISBN 978-0-8117-3604-6
    1. Turkey hunting. 2. Game calling (Hunting) I. Title.

SK325.T8H534 2009
799.2'4645—dc22
                                                            2008042906

Turkey calling history combines tradition and technology.

Turkey Calls and Calling is dedicated to the Native Americans who made turkey calls from wing bones for their subsistence hunting, and also to the modern callmakers who use up-to-date tools and materials to both converse with this amazing game bird, and to provide wild turkeys for their Thanksgiving tables and springtime barbecues.

This book honors all of them, past and present, and of course the wild turkey that callers and callmakers pursue. And yes, even now some twenty-first-century purists still craft and use homemade wing bone calls to speak that second language.

Contents

Preface

*T*urkey Calls and Calling provides the modern wild turkey enthusiast with a user's guide for speaking the language of this great American game bird. This book is not only an invitation to those of you who want to improve your basic calling skills, but also a thoughtful examination of the calling tradition that you veteran turkey hunters value as much as I do. What follows is my effort to share my thoughts and field experiences as a longtime wild turkey hunter, caller, and enthusiast. This comprehensive title examines many aspects of the turkey calling tradition—in both words and images.

You'll read about callmaking history. You'll learn about the variety of friction, air-activated, and locator calls that are used by approximately 3 million turkey hunters. You'll examine how to identify and make situational and seasonal vocalizations to effectively draw wild turkeys into gun or bow range during available spring, fall, and winter seasons. In these pages I also cover competition calling (an activity that's adjunct to hunting turkeys, but is of value in our complete examination of calls and calling), caring for your turkey calls, and finding callmakers. The appendix includes other callmaking resources.

Sure, you can tag a wild turkey without making any vocalizations. I have no problem at all with anyone who uses their woodsman's ability to pattern turkeys in order to put his- or herself in the right place at the right time without calling those birds to their position. It's legal. It's practical. And it often works.

Still, understanding turkey calls, as well as how, when, why, and where to use them, elevates your hunter's game to the highest level of interaction and meaning. Indeed, woodsmanship skills are important as you match vocalizations with wild turkeys during hunts.

That's why calling spring gobblers, and autumn or winter turkeys, can increase your enjoyment of the game: if you know how and where to find the birds, the desire to add basic or advanced calling to your hunting strategies is probably why you're now holding this book in your hands.

In the end, when you successfully converse with a spring gobbler, or autumn or winter wild turkey, you've crossed over into a meaningful realm unrivaled in the hunting tradition. When all is said and done, using manmade calls to talk with a wild turkey in the bird's own language, in order to lure that quarry to your setup position, is pretty amazing stuff.

Acknowledgments

Thanks to all the folks at Stackpole Books, but especially Judith Schnell who supported this project from the start (several informal Orlando, Florida, meetings at the 2007 SHOT Show) to the finish—the book you now hold in your hands.

Thanks also to all my editors, publishers, and colleagues in the outdoor industry, far too many to name here, but all of them important. Many of them are as affiliated with—and affected or afflicted by—the wild turkey as I am.

I'm grateful as well to all the good people in the turkey-calling and callmaking world for their assistance with this book, and all the folks I've shared turkey camps with around the country over the years.

The National Wild Turkey Federation also deserves mention for its ongoing pro-hunting conservation endeavors and educational projects and efforts regarding this great game bird. If you aren't a member, consider becoming one.

Finally, I have constant appreciation for my wife, Elizabeth, and daughter, Cora, and their ongoing patience with this book project, as with others I've crafted at this writing desk. It's the best lifestyle for me, but I doubt many spouses or children could put up with the challenge of a husband at his writing desk much of the time, or a daddy on the road hunting turkeys around the country for the rest of it.

I couldn't do this without all of you in my life.

Introduction:
The Calling Tradition

First, let's cover some necessary semantics.

As wild turkeys and word meanings go, a "call" can be a noun, denoting the actual device used to make vocalizations, or a verb, meaning the act of calling a turkey. In turn, a caller is both the person making the turkey vocalizations, and the actual tool used to do it. Calling, the act of using a call to draw a wild turkey into range, and also the strong intense desire to pursue this tactical advantage, are components of this tradition too.

Originally the need for using turkey calls was far more serious than wordplay. Since their survival depended on it, Native Americans crafted and used calls to lure the wary wild turkey into range. As practical subsistence hunters, necessity demanded this ingenuity, and their inventiveness yielded a turkey call by joining turkey wing bones together, then drawing air through the hollow device.

While archaeological excavations show that early callmakers used these bones, and even wood and stone among other useful available items, both manmade and natural materials are integrated these days. The modern outdoor industry continues to capitalize on this original ingenuity with variations and adaptations. Still, some modern throwback purists use only natural items, as a traditional archer might craft his own bow rather than opt for a modern, tricked-out compound.

There have been many callmaking manifestations, but in the end two kinds of turkey calls exist now as they did long ago: one requires air activation while the other needs friction. Nowadays, modern hunters have diverse personal collections of turkey calls, but they tend to fall back on their preferences. Though these vocal wild birds make upward of thirty different calls, in live hunting situations hunters usually use just a few calls. Still it's important to understand them all, and to know what you are hearing when you hear it.

The first hint that turkey calls were marketed as part of outdoor commerce arose in the late nineteenth century. In 1897, Henry C. Gibson

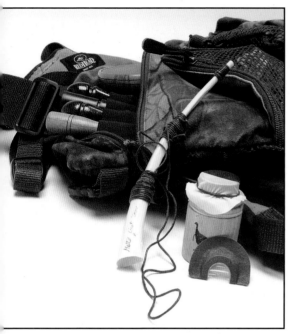

patented his box call. Subsequently his structural style—basically a hand-held, coffin-shaped, sound-chamber box operated by running the lid across either lip of one of two side panels—was varied by many callmakers, a trend that continues today. His rectangular box, particularly the innovation of attaching the paddle handle (the "lid") with a hinge screw, provided the prototype. The versatile box call has lasted into the twenty-first century, largely because it can be used to imitate all the many wild turkey vocalizations, including the gobble.

Calling history reflects other variations, such as cedar scratch boxes, cow and goat horn yelpers, slate calls paired with corncob-and-wood strikers (my first turkey call as a Pennsylvania teenager), and so on—all of these tools aimed at allowing the human caller to talk wild turkey. Native American wing-bone calls were the models for the Charles Jordan and Tom Turpin

There have been many callmaking manifestations, but in the end two kinds of turkey calls existed long ago as they do now: one requires air activation, while the other needs friction. Nowadays, modern hunters own diverse personal collections, but still fall back on their favorite pieces. A variety of calls can be used in the spring, fall, and winter turkey hunts.
NATIONAL WILD TURKEY FEDERATION

yelpers, among others, including the continued development of this call among certain modern callmakers.

Practicality insisted that a calling device be developed to allow the turkey hunter to call without using his hands. Advertisements for the earliest marketed mouth diaphragm calls, specifically the H. P. Bridges version from the 1920s, allude to the portability and easy operation of this tool—at least potentially, as mouth calls are the most difficult to master. The same qualities hold true these days for this calling tool, which is essentially latex stretched across the opening on a horseshoe-shaped frame.

Influenced by Gibson's innovations, enterprising Alabama callmaker M. L. Lynch began traveling in the 1940s to market his now-famous box calls to distant buyers. It's interesting to note that in Lynch's time, turkey hunting was only permitted in fifteen states, as opposed to a generous forty-nine now in the spring, and forty-four states in the fall and/or winter. Times have never been better for the conservation-minded turkey hunter using a call to take a bird.

Once outlawed as flock numbers dwindled nationwide, calling devices are now acceptable everywhere wild turkeys are hunted. Wild turkey hunters use examples from among their personal possessions, and even consider themselves collectors—either with deliberate enthusiastic effort, or as incidental accumulators of calling devices. A new call on the market always gets some attention, even after all these years of development. (Many examples surround me in my office as I write this . . . I play with calls on almost a constant basis. Crazy? Not to a turkey caller and hunter.)

These days, a blended combination of calling tactics and savvy woodsmanship, first initiated long ago by Native Americans using wingbone callers, is viewed as the modern sporting way to take a wild turkey. Modern callmakers—those who build friction calls in particular—often speak of their efforts to get many different turkeys inside of one particular call. In other words, the versatile box call should not only be able to provide decent clucks and yelps, the staple of any spring gobbler hunter's calling approach, but also produce such vocalizations as the *kee-kee* and *kee-kee-run* for autumn and winter turkey hunters.

Surely versatility rules, and often the cosmetic beauty—a byproduct of such calling tools—redefines these friction calls as vital American folk art with a direct function: calling wild turkeys. The lively nature of modern turkey hunters building their own calls continues to honor the original calling tradition.

These days, the outdoor industry caters to the modern wild turkey hunter by providing fairly inexpensive and highly functional options with which to call their birds in. Other more expensive, but equally effective, custom turkey calls are available to the buyer who wants not only the reliable function of a "pickup truck," but also the elegance of a "sports car."

In the end, it may only take one turkey call to tag a wild bird, but owning, using, and enjoying many of these devices adds to the ongoing experience as you personally extend the turkey calling tradition.

—Steve Hickoff
Kittery, Maine
April 2008

Wild turkeys are gregarious birds that respond well to calls—both those made by real gobblers and hens, and accurate vocalizations rendered with manmade friction and air-activated calls.

PART

1

Types of Calls

Friction,
Air-Activated,
and Locator

1

Friction Calls

Turkey calls are tools crafted to fool wild turkeys so that these highly vocal gamebirds come to your setup position expecting to encounter a hen, a gobbler, or turkeys of both sexes. Such deceptive measures define the art of turkey calling. This initial chapter—and the two that follow—will describe the kinds of friction calls available to you, the modern wild turkey hunter. Visual support in the form of photographs and drawings will offer you examples of the diverse types of friction calls from which you can choose, the many kinds of materials used to construct these devices, and each call's functional parts.

In the end, experience in the field while hunting wild turkeys, and while practicing at home when not, will allow the turkey hunter and caller to gain familiarity with these hunting tools. This intimacy is crucial to calling effectively. Running a turkey call in an indoor situation—say at a winter hunting show or in the privacy of your home—is one thing: field-testing that device on real turkeys is a start toward something better.

Accumulating an understanding of how, when, where, and why you use a turkey call has something to do with making all the mistakes you can when hunting and calling turkeys, and learning from game-time errors—even though such mistakes will likely be revisited from time to time, with unexpected twists and turns dealt by the bird in question. We'll deal with all of these call-related aspects in due time. First, let's take a general look at friction calls.

In short, friction calls require hand movement to create friction—friction being the simple notion of rubbing one object or surface against another. Properly rendered results create accurate vocalizations that fool turkeys.

Sometime way back when, early man rubbed two sticks together to make fire. Staying warm and eating were survival priorities. He also had to find a way to call wild game close enough to kill it. Calls were created to do just that.

Air-activated calls came before friction calls. Leaves from various trees and shrubs, when held just right and blown, were the most naturally available tools for early hunters. Native Americans fashioned wing-bone callers out of necessity. Archaeological records of these calls predate those in seventeenth-century America, before the arrival of European settlers.

Hand-operated friction calls were first developed in the nineteenth century, and some production took place, particularly in the latter half of the 1800s. The Gibson box established a standard you still see today. Such hunters as Tom Turpin and M. L. Lynch improved upon this prototype with their own adaptive models into the middle of the twentieth century. (Remarkably, during this time turkey hunting was only permitted in fifteen states due to diminished flock numbers.) Other friction calls emerged along the way.

The notion of rubbing one object against another to create turkey vocalizations (i.e., friction calling) prompted the use of animal bones, even turtle shells, as sound chambers to amplify a

The author with a high-meadow Merriam's longbeard taken on a recent Wyoming spring hunt.

wooden peg's sounds. Early strikers were often made of cedar or other woods, stroked across a slate face. Many surface and peg variations appeared historically, as necessity has always been the mother of friction-calling invention. Box strikers, scratch boxes, cedar scrapers, and others, such as slate/string/peg calls, were the result of a desire to render various turkey call vocalizations.

Friction calls, then as now, rely on one specific requirement: one element is stroked against another element to make a sound. The striker is as important as the striking surface on a pot. Ditto for scratch boxes. Box calls rely on the same idea, but wed the two parts with a hinge screw.

Strikers, pictured here with a slate call, come in many forms.

Back in the 1970s, when I first hunted turkey in Pennsylvania as a teenager, I carried a corncob-handled ash peg affixed with a string to a palm-sized slab of slate. My left hand (cupped around that slate) functioned as the sounding chamber. You may laugh, but that primitive version actually emitted clucks and yelps accurate enough to fool a few gobblers during my college days. It wasn't long before I moved on to other friction calls, though I still have that first one, which sits retired behind glass near my desk as I write this. Nostalgia? You bet.

Three developments accounted for the friction-call market's growth: (1) turkey numbers increased nationwide due to improved management; (2) turkey hunter numbers grew; and (3) friction call options exploded as competition raged (and still does). Suddenly, discriminating friction-call users had some style options, though slate calls have consistently ruled— still do for some. More variations followed.

Fast-forward to the mid-1980s and early 1990s when manufactured pot-and-peg, scratch, and box calls took a step forward—though the former type changed more than the latter two. During the 1980s, D. D. Adams glass-and-slate calls were the ground-breaking prototype for many of those examples seen today, two decades later. As with Gibson and his box, a solid design spawns many innovators. The use of more exotic wood is a current trend.

One thing you'll notice about the marketing of manufactured friction calls in the 1990s is the presence of more push-pull (or push-pin) options. Along the way, these received the unfair tag of "idiot boxes," suggesting that anyone can use them to make effective turkey calls (mostly true). However, advanced hunters will use tree calls, purrs (contented or fighting), and yelps (hen and gobbler), which can all be made with push-pull calls. Although these calls are easy to use, they are diverse in application.

As wild turkey numbers steadily increased nationwide from the early 1970s through the last years of the twentieth century and beyond, more hunters— some who may not have ever hunted turkeys because the population was once very low—took on the tradition. According to the National Wild Turkey Federation (www.nwtf.org), in 1973—the year this nonprofit, prohunting, management-savvy organization was founded—just 1.3 million wild turkeys were available to the 1.5 million sportsmen who considered themselves turkey hunters. Now 7 million turkeys provide opportunities for roughly 3 million turkey hunters in the United States and in parts of Canada and Mexico. D. TOBY THOMPSON/NATIONAL WILD TURKEY FEDERATION

As wild turkey numbers steadily increased nationwide during the decade of the 1990s, more hunters—who may have never hunted due to the low turkey numbers or unavailability of legal hunting—took on the tradition. As a result, the friction-calling market offered products that were functional, of a basic design, inexpensive, and practical, as well as well-crafted and more expensive versions.

Friction calls—pot-and-peg, scratch, and long-box versions—have developed dramatically in the last decade. Manufacturers began layering manmade materials for calling surfaces to create different sounds, a restless search that continues to this day. Aluminum-faced pots, which ring out on windy days and project great distances, have become popular options. Other surfaces were created to beat the moisture.

Friction calls can be loud or soft, depending on the situation. The sounding chamber amplifies the striker as models from the past did. But now you'll find a pot-and-peg for every situation; and the fact is, friction calls just keep getting better and better.

Some still think that you can't reinvent the friction call. But it must be hard for the cynics to argue with the advent of the waterproof friction call. Years ago, I wrote magazine and newspaper articles suggesting you should carry plastic bags to house your friction calls. That's still true for some calls, but now many prominent companies offer at least one waterproof model.

Accessories for friction calls have increased exponentially. You now have silencer straps to fit around friction calls that were once wrapped with rubber bands. (Note: rubber bands still work to quiet them.) You have tuners for pots-and-pegs, which help you "dress"—prepare for use with box chalk and sandpaper—glass, slate, aluminum and other surfaces, as well as your striker tips. You have hands-free holders for your pot-and-pegs to limit movement while shotgunning or bowhunting turkeys. You have special chalk that's applied to striker tips for use in damp and wet conditions, wristband conditioners for quick striker touchups, carrying cases, and perfectly shaped pockets to house friction calls in your vest.

Calling a turkey to your position, knowing that you've spoken the language of a wild bird, is particularly satisfying. More friction calls in your vest simply represent more turkey-calling variety. Times have never been better for the friction-call user.

Modern friction calls can be put into four categories: box calls (both short and long styles, with curved or straight paddles), push-pull (a.k.a. push-pin) calls, scratch boxes (with small hand-held strikers), and pot-and-peg calls that are functional when using a multitude of other striker options. There are many variations, ranging from purely practical to elaborately decorative, but we'll deal with the former four options here.

Best of all, friction calls are generally easy to use—a plus for both the beginning hunter and the veteran of the turkey woods.

Box calls—both short and long styles, with curved or straight paddles, as well as smaller push-pull calls—provide many options for the modern turkey caller.

Since a wild turkey answering your call can pinpoint the source of your setup with radarlike ability, friction calls can be used to draw that bird in while it's vocalizing to your calls but still out of sight, before you either switch to the hands-free diaphragm or go silent as the turkey seeks out your calling location.
NATIONAL WILD TURKEY FEDERATION

BOX CALLS

Box calls are slender, rectangular wooden boxes with gently arched sounding-board sides. The paddle (or lid) sits on top, and it is usually attached with a spring-wrapped hinge screw on one end. This lid's length extends to form a front handle, which is held when calling. By working the paddle's bottom against the box call's side lips, you can make the entire turkey vocabulary, including gobbles. Though box calls take up space, most turkey vests have a lengthy pocket to accommodate them.

Box calls require visible hand movement to operate them—a by-product of friction calling that paranoid wild turkeys can readily detect even at great distances. However, you can conceal a box call behind a raised knee or inside a blind, or you can simply use it comfortably when turkeys are out of sight.

Box calls should be held firmly along the sound board but gently on the paddle handle, either horizontally in your left palm as you work the lid with your right (southpaws reverse this), or vertically, with the front

Box calls should be held firmly along the sound board but gently on the paddle handle, either horizontally in your left palm as you work the lid with your right (southpaws reverse this), or vertically, with the front handle up and the screw end facing down. You can also run the box against the stationary paddle.

As with all game calls, it pays to practice regularly until you can render realistic wild turkey talk—especially in live situations while hunting.

handle held up and the screw end facing down. You can also run the box against the stationary paddle.

As with all calls, it pays to practice regularly until you can render realistic turkey talk. Each box offers different qualities. Boat paddles, or so-called long boxes, provide a greater contact length as you run the call.

Box calls can be made from walnut, furniture-grade mahogany, butternut, ash, yellow poplar, sassafras, cedar, mesquite, maple, wild cherry, and even so-called exotic woods, such as purpleheart and osage. They can even be made from recycled rail fences and barn wood, themselves fashioned from American chestnut, a tree dramatically diminished by blight in the early twentieth century, and now undergoing conservation-minded reintroduction efforts.

You should tune your call before you hunt as well, and even during the hunt, with friction-call chalk, though some modern-day models require no chalking at all. Some models are even waterproof, an asset on damp spring, autumn, and snowy winter days. Others still require that old-school protective approach of slipping them into a carrying case or no-frills plastic bag when afield during stormy outings.

Some hunters silence box calls while walking in the woods using rubber bands or wraparound hair ties stolen from unsuspecting spouses. Some manufacturers offer silencer straps to minimize noise as turkey hunters walk, and in the process minimize marital distress.

Modern box-call innovations now require no chalking at all and are even water-proof, an asset on damp spring, autumn, and snowy winter days.

PUSH-PULL CALLS

You push it. You pull it. It makes turkey sounds.

Some hunters refer to these calls as "idiot boxes," an unfair assertion, as these hunting tools require a certain finesse to use effectively. If such devices—also known as "push-pin" calls—aren't properly tuned or chalked, the results sound seriously deficient. Pull one out of the package, and you'll have to tinker with it at least a little bit.

Most operate based on a long wire inside the call that controls plunger tension. The plunger works the movable striking surface across the fixed striker to create turkey sounds. Callers can tweak this device if notes aren't quite right. Fiddle around. Get it right. Adjust between hunts.

Push-pull calls can be held and manipulated three ways. First, hunters typically run these calls by gently palming them while working the plunger with the index finger of the same hand, as if pulling a shotgun's trigger. I, however, prefer to cradle the call in my left hand, while pinching the plunger between my right thumb and index finger, softly stroking it up into the box. This technique is particularly effective for making sleepy tree calls to roosted wild turkeys before fly-down time.

I also use a third option: positioning the plunger's tip on my knee, I move the smallish push-pin call up and down to make clucks, yelps, cutts, cackles, and purrs.

Turkey hunters typically run push-pull calls by gently palming them while working the plunger with the index finger of the same hand, as if pulling a shotgun's trigger. You can also cradle the call in your left hand and pinch the plunger between your right thumb and index finger, softly stroking it up into the box.

Dummy? Idiot? I don't think so. Such push-pull calls have helped me kill many spring and fall turkeys over the years. I often use a push-pull device while I am also calling on a mouth diaphragm.

Push-pull calls typically are made of black walnut and have a carbon dowel striker rod or acrylic peg. While chalking the striking surface regularly maximizes this tool's potential, some recent models require no chalking and are waterproof.

Some models pair two calls together to simulate fighting purrs—the sound of two turkeys squaring off with pecking order at stake. Think of an Ali-Frazier fight back in the day. Using two push-pull calls at once replicates these battles. Some styles are even designed to attach to your shotgun barrel with clips; you operate these using a lanyard.

SCRATCH BOXES

So small they often fit in your shirt pocket, quiet until you use them, scratch boxes are hand-held friction calls, which operate on the same principle as a box call, but without the attached paddle. By gently holding the scratch box in one hand and the striker in the other, you can cluck, yelp, and purr. Some callers move the striker against a scratch box's lip (like the bigger box call, or boat paddle, it has two lips), while others move the scratch box against the striker's chalked wooden surface. The chamber's empty space between the two lips makes the sound.

Wooden materials used for scratch boxes include butternut, chestnut, bocote, cedar, poplar, and mahogany. Strikers need occasional chalking, but are otherwise low maintenance and pocket portable.

Some push-pull models are paired together for making fighting purrs—the sound of two wild turkeys like these gobblers squaring off with pecking order at stake. Think of an Ali-Frazier fight back in the day. Use two push-pull calls at once to replicate this. TIM SIMOS/NATIONAL WILD TURKEY FEDERATION

POT-AND-PEG CALLS

Most pot-and-peg calls are round with a striking surface, and require the use of a peg or "striker." Striking surfaces can be made of slate, glass, aluminum, and other manmade materials. Pegs can be wood, glass, carbon, or plastic. Some old-school callers even fashion strikers by gluing turkey wing bones to antiquated brass shotgun hulls. While manufactured pegs provided with the pot certainly work, you can experiment with a variety of strikers to render a different tone and volume for clucks, yelps, and purrs.

Striking surfaces must be roughed up (or "dressed") with so-called "scuff pads" to call properly. Sandpaper, or fine-grit drywall paper, works on glass surfaces and slates. Some callers use ScotchBrite scour pads on their traditional slate calls. Small squares of this material can be carried along on hunts for dressing pot-and-peg calls. Maintain the call's surface by gently sanding in one direction—four or five strokes works fine. Striker tips can also be treated with an emery board.

Pots are manufactured in a standard circular design, and are typically made of walnut, cherry, mahogany, cedar, osage, and cocobolo, or even plastic or other manmade composites.

Most pot-and-peg calls are round with a striking surface and require the use of a peg (also known as a "striker").

STRIKERS

Can you write with a pen or pencil? If so, you can run a striker.

A striker or peg is a tapered hand-held dowel or rod with a rounded tip that is worked across the pot's surface to render turkey vocalizations. Wooden striker materials include ash, cherry, birch, oak,

A striker or peg is a tapered hand-held dowel or rod with a rounded tip that is moved across the pot's surface to render turkey vocalizations.

walnut, locust, hickory, yellowheart, purpleheart, canary wood, teak, rosewood, zebrawood, osage, cocobolo, and bubinga, among others.

Some modern callmakers combine types of wood with different heads and shanks, or use materials that include acrylic and carbon. Carbon pegs matched with aluminum or glass surfaces will often work on damp or drizzly spring or autumn days when other strikers won't, but you can also use waterproof pot-and-peg calls. Variations in striker types include old-school corncob tops paired with modern glass, carbon, or wood rods. Brass shotgun hulls matched with a turkey's wing bone add creative interpretations.

FRICTION CALL SELECTION

Choosing turkey calls is a bit like picking a fly pattern, a lure, or even the best bait while fishing. With experience, you'll learn which calls work for you and which don't; still, you may find that something in you yearns to keep looking and trying out new offerings. The experimentation is half the fun.

There are several ways to go about making these choices. You can try out turkey calls and product examples at hunting shows to get a sense of

Proper striker and pot-and-peg form.

how such offerings sound. You can persuade your hunting buddies to loan you their friction calls, if only for a moment or two while afield. (It's funny though: friction call choices are as personal as a shotgun, fly rod, or other item of gear you might use—sharing them with buddies is uncomfortable for some, while others may not mind at all.) Finally, you can simply invest the money and time in acquiring many different friction calls—often far more expensive than air-activated diaphragms—indulging happily in your call-acquiring obsession, empty wallet notwithstanding. There are worse addictions, surely.

KIDS CAN TOO

Shortly after the release of my *Fall & Winter Turkey Hunter's Handbook* (Stackpole Books, 2007), I traveled from my home in northern New England to visit a retail store in Kansas to offer insights to customers on turkey hunting the autumn flocks. While there, I encouraged kids who had never touched a turkey call before to try them out. As usual, the results proved interesting.

I selected box and glass friction calls because of their ease of use, which I then dressed. I passed on talking about the more advanced diaphragm, which fits in the roof of your mouth. Using a mouth call is often difficult for even the practiced turkey hunter, a condition I aim to assist in this book. Nevertheless, with simple instruction on how to use the glass-faced pot—"Hold the striker like a pencil, keep it touching the surface, and draw little ovals or circles"—many of the kids produced decent yelps and clucks in just minutes.

Same situation with the box call: "Just hold the paddle lightly, and drag it across the call's lip or edge." Several parents cheerfully remarked as they looked on: "Grandpa has one of those," indicating, I assumed, that they didn't hunt turkeys. Not yet.

Of course, I oversimplify matters here. This sort of experience is just a beginning. Yes, the kids made turkey sounds. Interacting with a real turkey, the most paranoid prey on the planet, is another matter. That sort of experience comes with time. To become a turkey hunter—and competent caller of the birds—children and adults need to acquire a sense of call options available. They need to understand the range of turkey vocalizations, and how to use and make calls. Situations in which you find turkeys while hunting can be challenging too. That's why I wrote this book.

Apart from proving that youngsters (and often adults) enjoy nearly anything that produces noise, my seminars teach plenty: kids, given some instruction, can learn to make wild turkey sounds. Friction calls are easy to use, and if you encourage young hunters to engage in this calling tradition with positive mentoring, the results can prove favorable now and in the future.

I also suggested to the parents (wink, wink) that friction calls make great stocking stuffers, realizing that in some cases that job might still be Santa's secretive business.

Turkey calls hanging in bright holiday stockings above the fireplace? Better than those plush toys that utter psychotic babble, I say.

2

Air–Activated Calls

WING-BONE CALLS

For some purists, the experience of calling a wild turkey with a tool crafted from the radius, ulna, and humerus bones of a fall hen or spring gobbler they've previously taken is hard to beat. It connects such thoughtful callers and hunters with early calling history—both personal and traditional. It's a simple and meaningful experience in this age of excess and twenty-first century complexity.

First things first: before making the wing-bone call, you'll need to kill a wild turkey. Then, tagged turkey in hand, you'll need some old newspaper, paper towels, a plastic bag, a reliable knife, a hacksaw or similar cutting tool, a file, sandpaper, some pipe cleaners or wire, and a glue gun or similar epoxy distributor. You'll also need a family who puts up with your wild turkey ways. At any rate, to make a wing-bone call, follow these steps:

Step 1: Spread the newspaper on the tabletop or counter where you're working. Have the paper towels nearby. Put the turkey on the newspaper.

Step 2: Locate where the wild turkey's wing joint and body meet.

Step 3: Remove the wing from the turkey's body by twisting and cutting it free from the socket joint, careful not to break the bones in the wing. Watch your fingertips—I share this tip from personal experience. Obviously, you can choose to make two wing-bone calls at the same time, and if you want to do this, simply remove both wings.

Step 4: Once this is done, remove the bony wing tip with the radius, ulna, and larger humerus bone still attached.

Step 5: Gently scrape away the feathers and meat from the bones with a knife, and put all this in the plastic clean-up bag. You can now easily see the radius and ulna wing bones, which run parallel to each other in the wing's middle section and are still connected to the larger humerus bone. You can create structural and sound variations by using hen bones, gobbler bones, or wing bones from both sexes. In the end, it's your choice.

To begin making a wing-bone call, spread newspaper on the tabletop where you're working. Locate where the wild turkey's wing joint and body meet. Remove the wing from the turkey's body by twisting and cutting it free from the socket joint, careful not to break the bones. An October jake taken by the author during Maine's 2007 season provided this example.

Step 6: Separate the three bones. The radius (the thinner of the two middle bones), the ulna (the thicker of the middle two), and the humerus (the largest bone remaining) should be boiled for fifteen minutes or so. Watch attentively, as the longer bones boil, the more brittle they become.

Step 7: Carefully scrape the remaining cartilage and meat off the bones again with your knife. If you have an old toothbrush, preferably a smaller child's version, you can use that too.

Step 8: Cut off each end of all three bones with a hacksaw or other similar tool—just enough to expose the insides. Discard the bony ends.

Remove the bony wing tip with the radius, ulna, and larger humerus bone still attached.

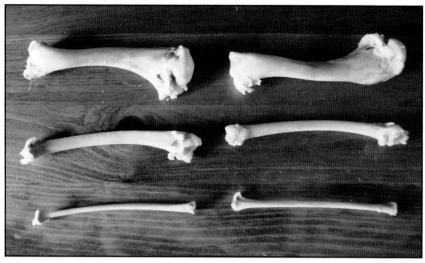

Separate the three wing bones. The radius (the thinner of the two middle bones), the ulna (the thicker of the middle two), and the humerus (the largest bone remaining) should be boiled for fifteen minutes or so. Watch attentively, as the longer bones boil, the more brittle they become. These examples are from two wings.

Inside the remaining bones you'll find marrow, which needs to be removed.

Step 9: Clean out the marrow inside each bone using a piece of wire or pipe cleaner.

Step 10: Using the tip of your knife, clean up the immediate interior end of each bone.

Step 11: Sand down or file the ends until they're smooth.

Step 12: At this point, you can boil the bones just a bit more or soak them in dishwashing liquid or an equal mix of water and bleach for several hours to brighten the bones.

Step 13: Dry the bones thoroughly, and pour yourself another cup of coffee.

Step 14: Study the bones a little. You'll see that the radius has both a rounded end and a flattened end. Handle the pieces a bit to get a feel for how they'll fit before gluing.

Step 15: Insert the rounded end of the radius bone into the ulna. Glue for an airtight fit and let it dry for several days. (Some callmakers stop here, as the radius and ulna bones alone can make clucks and yelps. Others add the humerus bone to the call for better sound projection.)

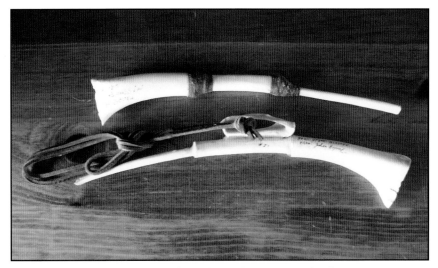

Several finished wing-bone calls from the author's personal collection.

Step 16: To add a third bone to your caller, insert the ulna's opposite end into the smaller tip of the humerus. Glue these two parts together, aiming for a tight fit. The third bone will amplify your calling.

Step 17: After drying again for several days, gently file off any rough edges, especially near the radius bone's mouthpiece end. Check the glue seals, and if they are airtight, your call is ready to use. Touch up with glue and sandpaper, or file as needed.

Some callers will inscribe memories of the hunts that put these turkey bones in their hands with permanent markers on the finished call; or if they've made the wing-bone call for a friend, they'll personalize it. Though such literal inscriptions may fade with time (a fixative may help), the memories likely won't. Others will brighten up the call with thread, paint, or a rubber lip stopper on the mouthpiece end. This ornamental aspect is often part of homemade grassroots callmaking.

Will domestic turkey bones work? Sure, though these bones typically have bigger holes, and lack the substantive personal value of using a real wild turkey.

MOUTH DIAPHRAGMS

Wing-bone calls link the past with the present. Some old-school turkey hunters use a practical approach to their calling by taking a blade of grass, cupping it in their hands, and blowing air past that natural reed (the shiny, leathery leaves of greenbrier were also used). But the modern

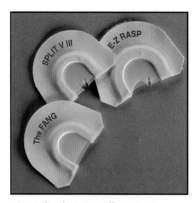

Most diaphragm calls are manufactured by modern industry callmakers and are predictably serviceable right out of the package. You may need to try several models to find the perfect fit.

HUNTER'S SPECIALTIES

turkey hunter often wants that functional ability contained in a small, portable device known as the mouth diaphragm. Most are manufactured by modern call-makers, and are predictably serviceable right out of the package. Some do-it-yourselfers make them.

Unlike friction calls, mouth diaphragms allow wild turkey hunters to call without hand movements, which the wild bird can easily spot with its keen eyesight. In certain situations, such as when spring gobblers or fall turkeys are approaching your setup, mouth diaphragms are the best option.

These air-activated devices are both inexpensive and easy to carry. Diaphragms are indeed versatile, though such calls are sometimes difficult for beginners to master. Even veterans have occasional trouble. At any rate, while it's true that a child could pick up a friction call and render acceptable clucks and yelps almost immediately, air-activated calls—which produce wild turkey sounds with air vibrations—provide a challenge.

As for diaphragms, some hunters can handle this foreign object tucked into the roofs of their mouths, while others have to fight down the gag reflex and simply cannot coax their unwilling minds around that mental obstacle. I've talked to turkey hunters over the years that opt instead for friction calls as a result of their discomfort with the diaphragm.

The construction of mouth diaphragms is fairly simple, though there are subtle distinctions among various manufacturers, and those structural differences influence the sounds you can make. Basically, mouth diaphragms are constructed by stretching latex rubber—often described in terms of a prophylactic reed—across a horseshoe-shaped frame centered inside a plastic skirt. The caller blows air across the latex reed (or reeds) to produce turkey sounds.

The appeal is obvious. They're so portable you can carry one inside your mouth while actively working a turkey in a live situation. They're so affordable you don't really need to worry about losing one—unless it sounded just right. They're so effective you can continue using lucky diaphragms until tooth marks fray the plastic skirt and the reeds go limp. I always have trouble throwing them away, and count hundreds among my personal possessions. (Seriously: my mouth calls are either old, fairly new, or in unopened packaging.)

Fact is, as I craft this particular chapter, the usual plans for fall turkey hunting are boldly marked on my office calendar. By all appearances I'll go afield with several new single- and double-reed diaphragms, including one or two gnawed versions I've used before to take autumn turkeys. Come spring I'll opt for calls that offer raspy hen yelps to draw gobblers into range.

While some might argue that a single-reed mouth call should be used by beginners, others feel the double-reed diaphragm is the easiest to handle, especially for making the *kee-kee* and *kee-kee-run* of young fall turkeys. As with turkey shotgun shells, it's best to try many before you settle on the perfect fit. The best personal diaphragm should allow you to

Mouth diaphragms are so portable you can carry one inside your mouth and use it in most situations you encounter in the turkey woods. Here Quaker Boy's late great Wayne Gendron calls a Texas Rio Grande gobbler.

seal that call tight against the roof of your mouth. A firm fit will make it easy to use the call.

As problems go, the aforementioned gagging reflex typically occurs when the mouth call fits poorly. Trimming the skirt on most diaphragm calls—sides first, then the back—can help. Take your time, and don't cut off too much material. I tweak mine using small fly-tying scissors available at many angling shops. Depending on the call or caller, some mouth diaphragms don't need to be trimmed at all. Smaller mouth calls are available to fit smaller palates, while others contain a built-in chamber that requires less air pressure to blow.

The author took these two New York State fall wild turkeys after his English setter, Midge, found and flushed the flock before the calling session. Diaphragm calls, which are great for making the requisite *kee-kees* and *kee-kee-runs* of young autumn turkeys, sealed this deal.

Assuming you've overcome these challenges, it's time to practice. Depending on your family's tolerance, you can do it indoors, settling for the acoustics of a remote garage, the second bathroom, or if banished elsewhere, your car or pickup truck as you drive to work or to hunt. By tape recording your mouth-calling efforts, you can work on improving your abilities to match these sounds. Call both indoors and outdoors to hear yourself. Live turkeys in their own habitats are often the best teachers of all. Get out there . . .

Manufactured diaphragm options these days include single, double, triple, notched, split, and stacked reeds. Stacked reeds are often matched with multiple frames to keep reeds from sticking together—a challenge for some mouth diaphragms after repeated use. Some reeds produce a high-pitch sound, while others offer raspy notes. Short of using the proverbial blade of grass, other old-school practitioners simply cluck and yelp with their natural voice, while others fashion homemade mouth calls.

Other air-activated devices include tube calls, trumpet calls, and gobbler calls. Some locator calls—addressed in the next chapter—qualify as being air-activated, but due to the diversity of options and locator calling use, they are covered in a separate section.

In the end, though, you still need to think and act like a wild turkey to talk like one.

TUBE CALLS

Fitted with latex single or double reeds, tube calls function somewhat like a diaphragm, but with the reeds contained on the call and used outside the mouth on the caller's lips. Air is blown past the reeds this way to render soft clucks, loud yelps for locating birds, and even gobbles.

Turkey calling history includes early examples made from snuff cans. Some modern manufacturers offer nostalgia-driven snuff tubes with slip-free reed systems. You can also make your own.

Step 1: Practical versions can be crafted from a plastic 35mm film canister, an object that is fast becoming a relic in these days of digital cameras. A plastic pill bottle also works.

No matter what call you choose, you still need to think and act like a wild turkey to fool a real bird, like this gobbler, into range with your man-made vocalizations. JOHN HAFNER/ NATIONAL WILD TURKEY FEDERATION

The snuff-can caller, a tube-call variation, is useful for making high-pitched cutting and excited yelping. Use it as both a locator call and to draw wild turkeys to your position.

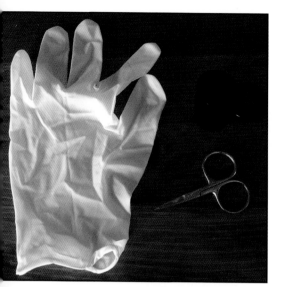

Some starter material for building your own tube call: medical-glove latex, scissors, and plastic tube.

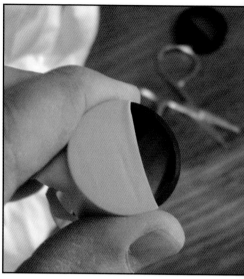

Cut a strip of medical-glove latex that you'll use to stretch across the open-ended top. This latex square should cover the lid as pictured here, with some hanging loosely over the edge.

Use a rubber band to hold the latex in place while you build the call.

Leave a thin opening between the uncut half-moon lid face and the latex edge. Keep that latex tight, and tune routinely by adjusting the cap and adding a fresh latex square.

Step 2: Remove the canister or pill-bottle bottom with a knife, hacksaw, or similar tool.

Step 3: Cut a strip of medical-glove latex that you'll use to stretch across the open-ended top on the other end. The latex square should cover the lid, with some hanging loosely over the edge.

Step 4: Cut the circular lid top into an open half-moon with your knife's tip, but retain the entire rim edge to allow you to snap the call into place.

Step 5: Snap the lid in place over the latex, and tighten the latex seal.

Step 6: There should be a thin opening between the remaining uncut lid face and the latex edge. Keep that latex tight, and tune routinely by adjusting the cap and adding a fresh latex square.

TRUMPET CALLS

Trumpet calls—both their shape and application—originate from wing-bone calls. Such lip-suction yelpers have a colorful history, a fact not lost on modern enthusiasts. Custom-made trumpet calls make up in traditional feeling what they lack in versatility. You can cluck and yelp with them. Some of the best callers can also *kee-kee* and *kee-kee-run* with them. As with the traditional tube call, this calling tool can locate a silent turkey, which is sometimes all you need to hatch a tactical approach to hunting it.

Modern callmakers have adapted some of the original trumpet-call prototypes to their own versions. Such wind instruments as the trumpet call can be effective in spring, autumn, and winter.

Callmaking contacts are listed in the appendix.

Ohio callmaker and turkey hunter Marlin Watkins demonstrates proper use of a lip-suction yelper.

Gobbler calls are air-activated, and contain three sections: the barrel, sounding chamber, and weighted bellow. Pictured here are models produced by Quaker Boy.

GOBBLER CALLS

Gobbler calls can lend variation to your typical cluck and yelp vocalizations. At times I think both spring and fall gobblers can be called with pure male turkey sounds, despite the fact that some hunters often only employ hen calls for spring toms. There's always some pecking order at stake, no matter what season you're hunting. It's often contested on a daily basis.

At any rate, gobbler calls are air-activated and contain three sections: the barrel, sounding chamber, and weighted bellow. Some feature attached volume-enhancing baffles on the end. These parts create a singular call: the male turkey's gobble.

Gobbler calls can be used just before or after morning fly-down to locate spring toms, or when male-only autumn gangs are regrouping after a flock bust. Gobbles can be tagged on the end of a *kee-kee-run*, as fall jakes will often call that way. This option is a good addition to your calling arsenal. Some hunters in the turkey woods—who have clearly crossed the species line—can even gobble with their throats and mouths.

3

Locator Calls

To call turkeys with either friction or air-activated calls, you first have to locate them. The so-called "shock gobble" is a condition mostly limited to, and typically linked to, the spring hunt. A male turkey, intent on breeding hens, sounds off to reveal its location so that female birds might come to it. That turkey might also gobble at other loud sounds it hears. Why is anyone's guess—they just do it. And we can make sounds to make them do it. Not always, but often enough that it's worth considering the range of locator calling tactics.

The so-called "shock gobble" is a condition typically limited to spring hunts. Locator calling is a hunting tactic that attempts to find a male turkey's unseen and silent position. BRIAN MACHANIC/NATIONAL WILD TURKEY FEDERATION

Favored by hunters, naturally occurring bird vocalizations such as owl hoots and crow caws are used to draw shock gobbles from springtime male turkeys. Here Eddie Salter of Hunter's Specialties uses a crow call to locate gobblers during an Alabama spring hunt.

In spring, when hunters target male turkeys, locator calls that imitate sounds other than turkey vocalizations are used to elicit the shock gobble. In spring, fall, and winter, wild turkey vocalizations produced with manmade turkey calls can draw responses from legal turkeys of either sex. You call. They answer back.

Naturally occurring bird vocalizations favored by hunters, such as owl hoots and crow caws, work to draw shock gobbles from springtime male turkeys. These are the two most common, traditional locator calls. Options abound. Unusual and unnatural examples also produce results.

Hunters can use this awareness of springtime male turkeys to produce sounds to induce shock gobbling. Those how-to calling strategies will be covered later in the book. For now, I'll survey the basic kinds of locator calling tools used in spring, fall, and winter seasons.

Types of locator calls for spring turkey hunting include:

Owl hooters: Most manmade versions allow for imitating the *who-cooks-for-you, who-cooks-for-you-all* call of the barred owl. This bird species shares the same habitat as the wild turkey, so the locator calling connection works. Some "owlers" are made of custom grade hardwood, and can be adjusted for louder, higher-pitched calling. Others, created with a more inexpensive design, provide adjustable reeds. Tone and pitch can be varied.

Crow callers: Manmade calls that work for crow hunting also draw shock gobbles from silent spring gobblers. Try a human rendition as simple as a plaintive *caw-caw-caw*. Examples range from well-crafted wood models to plastic versions. All can work in the hands of a proficient user.

Hawk screamers: The high-pitched sound of a hawk crying out can pull a location-revealing gobble from a male turkey.

Coyote howlers: These calls, which imitate the exact sounds of coyotes, definitely work to raise a spring gobbler's attention. On windy days a "song dog" howler can cut through the gusts.

Elk buglers: Autumn elk hunters who also chase springtime turkeys can use their calls two times a year. I've seen bugling work particularly well in western states such as Wyoming, even though the call is outside the autumn elk rut and used in springtime to locate gobblers.

Goose and duck calls: In

Demonstrated by Quaker Boy's Ernie Calandrelli on a Missouri spring gobbler hunt, a coyote howler imitates the exact sounds of a coyote, and can pull a shock gobble from a silent male turkey. On windy daybreak mornings a "song dog" howler can cut through the gusts.

spring, waterfowl flights are at the highest point outside of the autumn ritual. As a result, both honker and quacker vocalizations can draw gobbles from male turkeys.

Pileated woodpecker call: This bird commonly inhabits eastern wild turkey habitat, and its vocalization can produce shock gobbles.

Peacock call: Much like the pileated woodpecker call, the sounds of a peacock can draw gobbles from male spring turkeys.

Both friction and air-activated calls can draw a shock gobble response from silent male birds in the spring. The author took this 23-pound Texas Rio Grande gobbler that was first located with a box call, and pulled into range with the same call after repositioning.

Along with locator calls, both friction and air-activated options used to call wild turkeys can draw a response from silent birds in both spring and during the fall and winter seasons. How-to strategies for using locator calls follow in Part III.

When effective, locator calls pull gobbles from shut-mouthed spring gobblers, revealing their positions. Manufactured locator calls sound natural, but natural and unnatural

Spring gobbler hunters can use a full range of locator calls to find birds. Crow, hawk, owl, and coyote calls are pictured here.

sounds can shock a gobbler into sounding off, such as:

Woods and field sounds: The piercing call of a hawk high overhead can make a gobbler sound-off just as a manmade locator call can. The same goes for real crows, blue jays, pileated woodpeckers, geese, and other birds. In other words, you sometimes need to use manmade calls that imitate these individual birds to get a gobbler to sound off, but other times the real birds will do it for you. A woodpecker plucking bark off of a dead tree occasionally will draw gobbles from silent birds. Squirrels may elicit gobbles with their chatter, as may livestock bellowing in agricultural areas where you hunt spring gobblers. Listen as you hunt.

Suburban area sounds: Ironically, unnatural sounds can help you find birds. When hunting where sound carries from nearby suburban areas full of activity, listen for shock gobbles as a result of such things as dump-truck activity, factory noises, automobile horns, barking dogs, and so on. A nearby slam of a truck door might raise a bird. Rather than hunt a shock-gobbling bird directly from your position, use terrain to relocate. Let the woods settle down, ease in, and then begin working that gobbler.

Safety whistles: Loud and unnatural, safety whistles get your attention and that of spring gobblers too.

Ironically, unnatural sounds can help you find birds. When hunting where sound carries from nearby suburban areas full of activity, listen for shock gobbles as a result of such things as dump-truck activity, factory noises, automobile horns, barking dogs, and so on. This suburban Rio Grande gobbler will get a free pass today. NATIONAL WILD TURKEY FEDERATION

Loud safety or dog-training whistles will sometimes work to locate spring gobblers when other devices won't.

No matter what call you choose, first you have to know how to recognize turkey vocalizations. What do these sounds mean? Furthermore, when and why do wild turkeys make them?

PART 2

Wild Turkey
Vocalizations

4

The Turkey's Vocabulary

No matter what call you choose to use, you first have to know how to recognize turkey vocalizations. What do those sounds mean? When and why do wild turkeys make them?

Wild turkeys call to communicate in the wild, and almost any turkey sound the human hunter makes could lure a curious bird in for a look . . . or not. That's the calling game. Regardless, you need to interpret what you're hearing from live birds to successfully imitate them.

Biology teaches us that turkey poults begin to make sounds while still inside their eggs. Brood hens offer so-called "hatching yelps" to the peeping sounds inside those shells. This is how the bond between the brood hen and her charges is formed. It is the basis for all turkey calling—calls made between real birds, and your efforts to imitate the wild turkey's vocabulary. NATIONAL WILD TURKEY FEDERATION

Biology teaches us that poults begin to make sounds while still inside their eggs. Brood hens make hatching yelps to the peeping sounds inside those shells. And so it all begins. This is how the bond between the brood hen and her charges is formed. It is the basis for all turkey calling—calls made between real birds as well as your efforts to imitate the wild turkey's vocabulary.

Once hatched, the visual and vocal connection is made between poults and the brood hen. This link proves important for turkey survival. When a turkey calls and another one responds, the birds confirm visually that the sound is real. Turkeys wait to see the real bird before fully committing to moving. This hyper-paranoid tendency is crucial for a prey species to survive. It's why some gobblers stay at a distance, and it's also why you feel such a rush when they strut into range. Factor in the sounds turkeys make, the need to see real birds after hearing and making those vocalizations, and the inherent wariness of a prey species like the wild hen and gobbler and you have a great hunting challenge on your hands.

Wild turkeys communicate

When a wild turkey calls and another responds to it, a visual sighting confirms that vocalization is indeed real. As a caller and hunter, you can draw birds into range for a look if that first part is convincing enough. That's the essence of turkey calling. TOM EVANS/NATIONAL WILD TURKEY FEDERATION

alarm at a predator's real or perceived presence and vocalize a sense of well-being when all seems safe. Biologists, naturalists, and hunters of the wild turkey have noted many different vocalizations—over thirty, including distinct variations. Some hunters tag birds regularly with timely clucking and yelping. Others use as many calling strategies as possible. Look at an officially sanctioned National Wild Turkey Federation calling

Look at an officially sanctioned National Wild Turkey Federation calling contest judge's sheet and you'll see a variety of turkey calls listed there. Preston Pittman calls on a suction yelper during a recent competition. NATIONAL WILD TURKEY FEDERATION

contest judge's sheet, and you'll see the following calls listed there:

Cluck
Putt
Tree Call
Plain Yelp of the Hen
Cutting of Excited Hen
Adult Hen Assembly Call
Fly Down Cackle
Kee-kee-run
Purr
Caller's Best Call
Cluck and Purr
Gobble
Yelp of Excited Hen
Owl Hooting (sometimes done in a separate contest)
Gobbling (also sometimes done in a separate contest)

When you understand the turkey's vocabulary, your personal enjoyment of spring, fall, and winter turkey hunting will be enhanced. You don't have to use all the aforementioned calls, but knowing what they are in the woods when you hear them can help your hunting effort.

While scouting in summer you may hear a variety of turkey sounds—including those made by the brood hen to her charges, and vice versa. These calls linger into hunting season, changing as the family flock ages. The connection is strong, as the young turkeys need to honor the brood hen's instructions.

The hen's genetic desire to watch over a growing brood continues well into the autumn hunting season. This bond is a major factor in survival, and it's reflected in the hen's vocalizations as these birds mature. Fall and winter calling includes the brood hen's assembly yelp, along with the juvenile turkeys' *kee-kee* and *kee-kee-run*.

FAMILY FLOCK CALLING

Poults peep. Brood hens softly yelp back. As the flock grows, other calls emerge. Survival rules.

The alarm scream: it can be made by the poult if the young bird is distressed, or evoked by a brood hen when that turkey senses trouble. I've heard the latter call on several occasions while training leashed bird-dog pups in summer. Once, my English setter Radar went on point. I saw nothing in the tall grass. I moved closer to my dog, and suddenly a brood hen rose out of the concealing cover, the sound of unseen poults calling at her feet. She dropped her

Your personal enjoyment of spring, fall, and winter turkey hunting can be enhanced as you begin to understand the wild turkey's vocabulary. You don't have to use all the calls to hunt effectively, but identifying the many sounds in the woods and fields when you hear them can help your hunting effort. PETER D'URSO/NATIONAL WILD TURKEY FEDERATION

While scouting in summer you may hear a variety of turkey sounds—including those made by the brood hen to her charges, and vice versa. The connection is strong, as the young turkeys need to honor the brood hen's instructions; their survival often depends on it. TOM EVANS/NATIONAL WILD TURKEY FEDERATION

wings, approached. We backed off as she wailed and screamed, wings drooping, ready to attack.

The alarm putt: This call is made by the brood hen to insist poults remain on alert, preferably hidden. It's much like the putt that a turkey would make on detecting you seated at the base of a tree.

The assembly yelp: This call is a variation on the plain, lost, and tree yelps, which I'll cover shortly. It's made by the brood hen either to gather the flock on the ground at morning fly-down time, or following the separation of brood members by a predator (including the human hunter). The six- to twelve-note assembly-yelp call—I've heard even more notes in some situations—draws the young turkeys to the brood hen from wherever they have been dispersed. Each hen is different. Some sound like yapping dogs. Some could win a sanctioned calling contest. Nevertheless, each juvenile bird can identify the individual hen's voice, which makes it difficult to imitate the assembly yelp in a fall hunting situation, though occasionally you get lucky and call in the brood hen.

Brood bosses sometimes challenge other imposters in the woods. I've even seen autumn adult hens strut on several occasions in a posture of dominance. In this situation, it's often best to stand in sight and spook the brood hen to silence her—unless of course you want to legally take that bird. It's your decision in either-sex hunting situations. If you choose to

As a wild turkey flock ages, the *kee-kee* and *kee-kee-run* calls become part of the young turkey's emerging vocabulary. HENRY ZEMAN/NATIONAL WILD TURKEY FEDERATION

run her off, you can imitate the calls of young turkeys, specifically the *kee-kee* and *kee-kee-run*, and pull one of those juvenile birds in.

The *kee-kee,* and *kee-kee-run*: The *kee-kee* call is the maturing lost whistle of the young turkey transitioning in the fall. It's three notes, and roughly two seconds long. The *kee-kee-run* includes these three notes, with yelps added on the end (that's the *run* part). Four to ten notes might compose the *kee-kee-run*, which is about six to seven seconds long. When separated from their flockmates and regrouping, young autumn gobblers will often call with a *kee-kee-run*, and a gobble tagged on the end. Some might *kee-kee*, yelp, gobble, *kee-kee*, and yelp again in growing urgency. Calls vary. As I'll repeat over and over to anyone who'll listen: wild turkeys are the best teachers. Get out there and listen to them.

Following their morning fly-down from the roost, or after being flushed out by a predator, young turkeys often reassemble together first, then move in small groups to greet the hen as she makes assembly yelps. A highly talkative bird when lost, wild turkeys sometimes call repetitively as they approach another vocal juvenile hen or gobbler. That's why you can mimic a young turkey during a fall or winter hunt and pull that bird into range much easier than trying to imitate the brood hen. In spring, you may hear a young hen *kee-kee* as well. Occasionally, I've heard yelping and *kee-keeing* by the same spring hen.

As turkey hunters, we need to understand this family-flock language, and to interpret what it means when we hear turkey vocalizations in the woods. Even the turkey's yelp is multifaceted.

YELPING VARIATIONS

Yelping variations can be heard in both female and male turkeys. Made year-round, the tree, plain, and lost yelp—like the brood hen's assembly yelping—are often specifically situational. Hen and gobbler yelps also vary.

Tree yelping: Tree yelps are made with a series of soft sounds when the turkey is on its morning roost. Turkeys seem to make this sound to determine the position of branch-sitting birds in the flock before fly-down time. Hens usually make this short call with three to five notes. Soft clucking might be part of this initial calling to greet the new day. Male fall and winter turkeys may simply gobble on the roost as they do in spring.

Plain hen yelping: Roughly three to eight notes long, this is the calling option most often employed by spring turkey hunters to lure gobblers into range. As with other vocalizations, turkeys make it to indicate their position. The spring, fall, and winter turkey hunter can hear it from individual female birds, including those turkeys in broodless autumn hen

Lost hen yelps are louder and longer in duration than plain yelps. When separated from flockmates, turkeys of either sex sometimes call with loud, repetitious vocalizations. NATIONAL WILD TURKEY FEDERATION

flocks. Hen yelping is higher-pitched than the deeper, coarser yelping of gobblers. Tom turkeys yelp with a slower cadence, and yelps are generally fewer in number (in my experience, often three notes: *yawp, yawp, yawp*).

Lost hen yelping: These calls are louder and longer in duration than plain yelps. When separated from flockmates, turkeys of either sex sometimes call with loud, repetitious vocalizations. I've often heard lost yelping from scattered, broodless adult hen flocks in the fall. Spring hens will make this call as well. They call urgently until visual contact is made, then go silent on getting back together. Autumn gobblers will yelp and sometimes even gobble to indicate their location when separated.

Gobbler yelping: Gobbler yelps are deeper and have a slower cadence than higher-pitched hen yelps. The yelps are generally fewer in number, often just three notes. Friction calls imitate gobbler yelps best, though resonant diaphragms also work. Often three deeper, slower yelps—*yawp, yawp, yawp*—will get a so-called "super jake's" (one-and-a-half-year-old male turkey) or mature gobbler's interest during fall and winter hunts. Like the cluck, it's a questioning call that seems to say, "Where are you? I'm right here." I've also called in spring gobblers using gobbler yelps.

Once on a Memorial Day hunt in northern New England, I gobbler-yelped on an old slate call after catching a glimpse of red in the plowed cornfield through the cover of a green, leafed-out woods. Not long after, the turkey gobbler yelped back, moved deliberately into the area where I'd set up, and I closed the deal. That late-May bird wore three beards.

FLY-DOWN SOUNDS

Fly-down cackling: This sound is made as the turkey rapidly wings down out of its roost tree. It can range from several to nearly several dozen notes, depending on the distance the bird flies to hit the ground. Breaking branches as feather tips brush and claw through trees adds to the listening experience. It may even indicate the direction of flight to other turkeys—and to the human hunter. If you've ever heard and witnessed this call, you've seen the turkey steady itself on a tree branch, maybe clucking as it did so. Then as the bird crouched to fly, you may have heard another cluck or two before the turkey pushed off to take wing. After seeing this, you likely heard a mix of notes, from clucks to excited airborne yelps—maybe even a dozen or more. Sometimes wild turkeys only make a few sounds as they fly down and cackle. They sometimes make fly-up cackling when preparing to roost.

Fighting sounds: Sometimes right after fly-down, you may hear turkeys fighting. Gobblers definitely do it in all-male flocks as they sort out the pecking order. By making aggressive purrs, cutts, and gobbles, you can convince male birds to approach. This can also illicit fighting rattles. Just as a crowd gathers during a street fight to see what's going on, gobblers will investigate the location where such sounds indicate fighting wild turkeys. You can hold the lid of your cap and smack it against a tree or your leg to imitate wings colliding as you call with clucking, purring, cutting, and gobbling—as long as the turkeys are out of sight, and won't see your movements.

PITTING, PURRING, AND PUTTING

Clucking: When looking for flockmates or other lone hens and gobblers, wild turkeys cluck. This behavior is an effort to get another bird to step into view, and is made by a turkey as if to ask, "Where are you?" In a spring, autumn, or winter hunting situation, turkeys will often cluck on the approach, especially if you are clucking back or making another call. Gobbler clucks are low pitched when compared to a hen's. Clucks for both sexes can be spaced out, often two to three seconds or more between calls. Sometimes the turkey might make just one, and it may be soft or loud, depending on the situation.

Pitting: A kind of high-pitched clucking, this call can be heard if the roosted turkey flock is disturbed by a predator, perhaps even by you moving or sitting beneath them.

Purring: This year-round call, which ranges from soft to rather loud, reflects the turkey's level of tolerance and even irritation among other birds feeding or fighting. By analogy, it's like the soft, short growl of a

When looking for flockmates or other lone hens and gobblers, wild turkeys cluck. It's an effort to get another bird to step into view, and is made by a turkey as if to ask, "Where are you?"
NATIONAL WILD TURKEY FEDERATION

dog bent over its food bowl when another canine approaches. Dominance rules in the wild, and situations change with the seasons. For turkeys to feed in a properly dispersed way in a wood full of acorns or food plot full of chufa, they have to let each other know their whereabouts. Purring does this for both gobblers and hens alike. Hunters cagily approaching an area might detect the presence of turkeys by listening for purring. In the turkey woods, you can hear a broad range of loud gobbling and soft purring; some calls are subtle, some shockingly loud. Purring seems to imply contentment while turkeys move through a food source.

Alarm putting: This sharp *pock* sound is made when the turkey detects possible danger— most every veteran wild turkey hunter has heard this call with a sinking of demoralized heart. Like the cluck, it's used to get the attention of another bird. This uneven, single-note call broadcasts suspicion in the turkey woods. If you hear it when before there was silence, it means the turkey saw you before you detected it. An alarm putt might be a directive made by a brood hen to silence her juvenile flock. (Poults can putt at a young age.) The call is a directive to the predator indicating the hunting game is over. Does it work? Ask yourself: How many times have you given up on that turkey after hearing it?

The cluck and putt are similar. It's safe to say that a turkey looking for you and your calling position is clucking, while one that has just agitatedly flicked its wings and turned to walk away is putting. Body language and turkey posture sometimes define the sound.

CUTTING AND GOBBLING

Cutting: Also called loud clucking, this call is sometimes used by turkeys after fly-down, when the regrouping flock is on the ground but still visually separated. It can also be sounded by one calling turkey as it stands in place any time of the day, while another insistently yelping bird approaches its position. The lost turkey often goes to the stationary bird, which may be in a flock. Sometimes the opposite occurs as the group of birds moves to meet the solitary turkey. Many turkey hunters have called cutting hens to their position by mimicking the calls of that fired-up bird. Sometimes you can interest a hen with your enthusiastic calling—gobblers too. There's a chance that the whole flock will move toward you. At least you may have identified some huntable turkeys if one answers you this way.

Gobbling: In the spring, a gobbler is primarily attempting to call hens to his roosted or ground-standing position for breeding. In the fall and winter, he's declaring his proud presence, and he may gobble during daily efforts to maintain or improve his pecking-order status. Or gobblers may just be trying to locate one another.

This call might be heard early in the New Year as weather warms. This pre-mating period, in the northern winter, foreshadows the time when hens are ready to breed. Down south, in places like Florida, the breeding ritual starts in February, and varies throughout the country. As I was writing this book, I heard my first gobble on March 9. That flock included longbeards, jakes, and hens. Other years I've heard birds sound off during January thaws. By March 30 this past year, I heard gobbling in several southern Maine locations, though the season wouldn't commence for weeks. At the same time, friends down south were hunting gobbling Osceola turkeys.

Later on, even as breeding time passes and hens begin to sit on nests, gobbling continues. It can linger well into late spring and early summer in some parts of the country, like Maine.

In my experience afield—whether it be conditioning my bird dogs in summer or simply being outdoors where wild turkeys live—I hear gobbling from January to late June, and on slate-colored November and December mornings. Gobbling nearly ceases during the summer molt. By September you may hear it again, and most definitely in October when we fall turkey hunters spend more time in the woods. Basically, it's a year-round call, with high peaks and deep valleys.

Between gobblers' anticipation of spring breeding season and their intense urge to establish pecking order with male birds on an almost daily basis, gobblers generally call year-round with varying degrees of

In the spring, a gobbler is primarily attempting to call hens to his roosted or ground-standing position. STEPHEN BAUER/NATIONAL WILD TURKEY FEDERATION

intensity. In fall and winter, strutting gobblers spit and drum just as they do in spring—a *pfft, dummm* sound. This too is a close-range call that other turkeys hear if in range.

Though some southern hunters I've talked to seem to hear gobbling and see strutting less in autumn and winter, here in the north it's not all that uncommon. I watch turkeys year-round, take notes on their behavior, and enjoy the scouting as much as the hunting.

One southern Maine Thanksgiving week, with the temperature just above freezing, I glassed a large flock of wild turkeys in a pasture corner. The mega-group of birds consisted of brood hens, juvenile turkeys, and three full-fan strutters. Quite the sight. Clearly they were grouped together in pre-winter mode: family flocks and adult gobblers alike, with the toms jostling for pecking order, and the young birds feeding with the brood hens.

In hunting situations, I've also heard intense autumn and winter gobbling while calling all-male turkey flocks back after scattering them. I defy any turkey hunter to tell me this isn't just as exciting as what the spring hunt offers. Fixed on the flush site and drawn to it by the calling of other members of that gang of toms and/or jakes, it's hard to beat the intense thrill of gobbling coming from all directions. The birds cluck. They yelp. They make a wonderful racket.

But sometimes they seem to speak in the equivalent of human whispers.

CLOSE-RANGE VOCALIZATIONS

The late-September day dawned crisp and cool, with a blue sky above, and a gang of gobblers roosted to my north. Bow in hand during the archery-only New Hampshire fall turkey season, I listened intently and heard actual gobbling (some of you who don't believe they gobble outside of spring just cursed me, but it's true—get out there and listen). I'd been studying these birds, watching them, patterning their movements. I sat crouched inside concealing cover on a field edge where they cruised for early-fall insects and waited.

Soon they appeared: one, then the other four, cruising my way. I nocked an arrow, stifled the jumpstart in my heart, and waited some more. Soon they'd be in range—maybe.

Not so. They eased past me, out of sight, and out of range. More waiting. In time, they doubled back, still out of range, passing out of view on the other side. I laid my bow down, made ready to rush them for the flush. This fall-hunting tactic would put me in a position to call the scattered gregarious gobblers back together, once dispersed.

As they fed near the field edge past my setup, I ran in, flushing all five into the woods. One went one way, two went another, another bird hooked back past me, and yet another ran down the field. Not bad. Not bad at all.

Right now some of you are thinking that those gobblers might not get together for a day or so because that's what you've heard about fall gobblers—and maybe that's what you've seen too. I certainly have seen that on occasion. But in this case, I got lucky. They were gobbling hard, trying to regroup within the hour.

Gobbling in this situation has nothing to do with close-range vocalizations, for sure. It's loud. Rowdy. Urgent. I loved it—I was there to try and arrow one too. I heard them working back to the flush site, so I waited some time as the birds went silent—I assumed now they were together. I leaned forward and slowly peeked out on the edge of the woods to see all five moving single file toward my position, right along the field edge. Now they might appear too close.

The *chump and hum* is an unmistakable close-range sound made by strutting male turkeys. Sometimes it's called a *spit and drum*. The sound is created by a gobbler breaking into strut, with tail fan fully spread. ALBERT LAVALLEE/NATIONAL WILD TURKEY FEDERATION

They did. With my compound bow drawn right around the time I thought they'd appear, I held my seated stance, arrow ready, arms trembling a bit, locked in for my release. That's when the first gobbler popped up into view, no more than a foot or two from my broadhead as I sat in concealing edge cover. Call it turkey fever, or logistical confusion, but I did nothing. The gobbler paused, turned its long neck and purred something into the ear of the male turkey in line behind it. I know, because I saw and heard it. In the time it takes to whisper, "Let's get out of here," all turned and ran down the field edge, and cut back into the woods. I never made contact with them the rest of the morning.

Strange? You bet. And if I hadn't been there to witness it, I might doubt the story too. Thing is, it's true. Every word of it. At the risk of anthropomorphizing, that lead gobbler said something to the turkey behind it, and whatever it was, it was a warning.

Close-range vocalizations like this one inform the wild turkey vocabulary. Listen for the peeping of poults, and the brood hen's softly yelped response, and other calls too. Some, like the one just detailed, haven't even been named. Others include:

Lost call whistle: This three-note call is made by younger poults in summer when lost. I've been fortunate to hear it on many occasions while spending time in areas I've hunted in the spring.

Soft purring: The range of this call can be loud to soft—barely detectable at times.

Roost pitting: Though high-pitched, roost pitting isn't loud. I've heard it after blundering into both spring and fall turkey roosts. This sharp clucking no doubt alerts other turkeys in the group. It indicates that you, the predator and interloper, have been detected.

Chump and hum: Strutting gobblers make this sound. Sometimes it's called a "spit and drum." To recreate it to someone in turkey camp as you tell the story of your day's hunt, you might say, "*Pffft, duuuuum.*" That's how it sounds. The act of a gobbler breaking into strut, tail fan fully spread, creates it. To hens (and human hunters) it's a pairing of sounds that indicates a gobbler is nearby. Gobbling may follow it.

While some spring hunters rely almost entirely on the gobble to locate male turkeys, and scratch their heads when birds shut down and go silent, the spring, fall and winter enthusiast must listen for the range of turkey sounds in the woods—assuming the birds are talking.

SILENT TURKEYS

Wild turkeys can transition from being rowdy groups of vocalizing birds to going as silent as fog moving through the hills. Sometimes turkeys don't call at all. On other occasions, you might just hear them fly down in the morning, and wing up to roost at night.

In such silent situations, woodsmanship—and noting tracks, droppings, and other available sign on the ground—will help you find silent birds. I've called up spring and fall wild turkeys that have never answered back by knowing that they were nearby, though tight-beaked. Individual turkeys may softly cluck or yelp nearby at hearing your footsteps in the leaves—a muted effort, perhaps, to identify the approaching noise, and draw a

Turkey tracks on a muddy Texas Hill Country ranch road in April.

Wild turkey droppings, pictured here, indicate the presence of silent gobblers and hens. NATIONAL WILD TURKEY FEDERATION

response from the maker of that sound. They're wary. They only call when necessary.

In the end, you need to actively listen while scouting and hunting to distinguish isolated turkey sounds from other outdoor noises. Some of those other wildlife sounds might indicate that wild turkeys are passing nearby. Between the desire of a wild turkey to stay alive (an urgency reflected in many of their calls) and the gregariousness of these birds wishing to get together, you may hear a range of vocalizations in the turkey woods and fields where they roam.

STOP, LOOK, LISTEN

The best path of study is to get out there and listen for them.

Whether turkeys are vocal or not, spring, fall, and winter enthusiasts need to translate a diverse range of sounds into meaningful information for locating flocks and individual turkeys they want to pursue.

While the springtime sportsman (for whom the gobble might be the only thing he or she listens for) would certainly benefit by diversifying his or her listening strategies when afield, the woodstove-month hunter depends on it. Some sounds to listen for are from vocal turkeys. Some include non-calling noises that indicate hens and gobblers are nearby.

First, slow down and settle yourself. Turn off the CD that you've been singing to on the way to the woods. Cut the engine. Step out and close the truck door slowly so it quietly snaps shut. Take a deep breath. Clear your mind of the bills you need to pay and that lawn you need to mow. You're in the turkey woods now.

No, this isn't a twisted take on New Age philosophy, but you can't go stomping into the woods and hear turkeys effectively. To listen well, you've got to move along slowly and surely, attentive and calmly focused. Ignore the vehicular traffic on the distant highways. Turn off your cell phone. If it's October, you may note the humming of field insects, and crows cawing overhead. If it's April, you may hear various regional or migratory songbirds. Relax. Now listen for the sounds within this outdoor noise to hear the quarry you're after.

Approach likely habitats such as farm fields, clearcuts, power lines, and ridges from a downwind position. You might catch the purring of feeding turkeys and other soft calling this way. You may hear a far-off springtime gobble. On excessively windy days, focus your attention on river bottoms and draws where autumn flocks and spring gobblers with hens can get out of the blowing gusts, and you can hear more clearly.

To listen well, you have to be quiet yourself. Alone, it's not too hard. When hunting with a buddy, it's much tougher. Keep small talk to a

While some springtime sportsmen rely almost exclusively on the male turkey's gobble to locate legal birds, the autumn wild turkey hunter often listens for a diverse range of vocalizations where hunting birds of either sex is permitted, including those made by fall longbeards like these. MASLOWSKI/NATIONAL WILD TURKEY FEDERATION

minimum or you may miss sounds you need to hear to hunt effectively. When listening for turkeys at fly-down time with a friend, move some distance away and sit apart. Do the same thing when turkeys are flying up to their roost. One of you may pick up noises or see something the other person doesn't. The sounds you hear in the woods tell a story. Naturally occurring noises can help you hear and locate turkeys.

Turkeys and crows seem to have a long history of annoying each other. I've seen wild turkeys chase crows out of fields. At breeding time, crows certainly raid brood-hen nests. And it's no secret to spring enthusiasts that a crow call can be used to draw shock gobbles from male turkeys as a means of locating them. I've used crow calls all over the country to locate spring gobblers.

Squirrels routinely bark at turkeys passing nearby, scolding the movement of most any creature in the woods beneath their treetop views. Listen for agitated squirrels, especially if you suspect a turkey is on the approach. Crows call loudly in the presence of flocks, and they even dive-bomb groups of birds when asserting territorial dominance. Sometimes the cawing interlopers gather in tree-held groups above turkeys. This harassment is curious to the naturalist and hunter, and might occur for a variety of reasons.

I've had both squirrels and crows indicate the presence of nearby turkeys on hunts around the country. Blue jays and other birds sometimes grow agitated when turkeys are near too. Active listening helps piece together the turkey-hunting puzzle.

Hearing the sounds of turkeys fighting for dominance is another way to find birds. Leaves rustle as wild turkeys jostle for position. Wings slap and pop. Leathery necks twist, coiled in agitation. Bearded chests collide in a show of gobbler strength. Welcome to the daily fight for pecking order, which often begins

Crows and other predators sometimes raid turkey hen nests such as this one. Flocks of crows will occasionally harass turkey flocks as well. Crow calls are used around the country to draw shock gobbles from silent male turkeys.
NATIONAL WILD TURKEY FEDERATION

Audio Resources

Apart from actually getting outdoors and listening to real wild turkeys, the following resources afford callers and hunters an opportunity to hear recorded vocalizations:

Sounds of the Wild Turkey, provided by the National Wild Turkey Federation (1-800-THE-NWTF; www.nwtf.org) includes turkey vocalizations at daybreak, plus specific recordings of real birds clucking, putting, tree calling, plain yelping (hen), cutting (hen), adult hen assembly calling, fly-down cackling, *kee-kee-run*ning, purring, and clucking/purring flock talk. Owl hooting, a spring gobbler locator call, and gobbling are also provided free of charge with your online service, though NWTF memberships are strongly encouraged for all turkey callers and hunters.

Callers and hunters are encouraged to attend the NWTF's annual convention, which includes the Wild Turkey Bourbon/NWTF Grand National Calling Contest, an event that brings the best turkey callers in the world together in competition. NWTF Grand National Intermediate and Junior Calling Championships are also included.

The NWTF Custom Callmaking Competition takes place at this yearly gathering, representing the art and craft of making calls, as callmakers come together to represent their talents.

Midwest Turkey Call Supply (1-800-541-1638) provides one of the most comprehensive selections of classic and contemporary instructional turkey calling DVDs, CDs, and cassettes from a variety of outdoor industry professionals at R.R.3, Box 354D, Sullivan, Illinois 61951 or www.midwestturkeycall.com. It is a highly recommended resource for these educational aids and actual turkey calls, from custom to industry models. Catalog available.

Renowned turkey biologist Lovett E. Williams Jr. provides a wide range of wild turkey audio recordings generated from years of field study on his www.turkeyhuntingsecrets.com website.

During the spring gobbler seasons, which run from March through late May nationwide, www.realtree.com posts recent and vintage video footage that includes audio of hunters calling wild turkeys to their setups with specific regional offerings. The multimedia website provides the material in archived form as well, plus articles on the subject of wild turkey hunting.

right after male birds land on their feet after fly-down. A gobbler brawl can sound like two kickboxers sparring in the ring. Beaks peck and throats purr, and feet and spurs fly through the air, while other turkeys look on. Even hens contest for rank within a flock. You can listen for it, and often pinpoint the direction of the group's movements. I've heard these fights on numerous occasions during hunts, even when the turkeys weren't calling much.

Sometimes you simply hear turkeys walking—not calling, just covering ground. Listen for footsteps in the leaves and/or snow, depending on the season or location. Do this especially after you've made some initial contact with birds, or suspect one is close. I once hunted Wyoming spring gobblers in eight inches of May snow.

Safety rules, as always. Footsteps approaching your position could be those of a squirrel, a turkey, or maybe another hunter. Err on the side of caution. Make a final visual confirmation of the sounds you hope will materialize into a turkey.

In addition to footsteps made while walking, leaf scratching might signal that turkeys are feeding nearby. Soft purring (a close range sound), which often accompanies that activity, will confirm it. Depending on how close they are, you can either call to the birds, reposition on them, or wait for the turkeys to ease within shot range.

And don't despair if you hear a gunshot during turkey season. Make a mental inventory of the wild game that's in season when you hear a shot. In spring, it's often at a gobbler, or perhaps at a coyote that wandered in to turkey sounds, or simply at a target. In fall and winter, it could be a range of game birds and animals, depending on if the shot was fired by a rifle or shotgun. Either way, if you think the gun blast was likely made by a turkey hunter, stay put. Scattered birds might wander into your area. You might be able to call up a single bird that's been dispersed from the noise of the shot.

If a buddy is on the next ridge and likely took a bird (or tried to), sit tight. You might be able to celebrate together with your own turkey in hand. By all means, such hunters should work out a system of meeting up again during a hunt. Safety demands it. Don't ever make turkey calls as you approach his position. That's a no-brainer, right? You can regroup by owl hooting on the approach, or use another bird or animal sound readily identifiable to your friend. Sometimes it just makes sense to whistle. Walkie-talkies (where legal) or cell phones (service depending) can connect you, but these devices inhibit listening abilities.

Shooting sports can seriously damage your hearing. A recent visit to my audiologist confirmed I'd lost some hearing in my left ear, likely the result of being a right-handed shotgunner since I was twelve years old. (I was right-handed before that too, but couldn't legally hunt in Pennsylvania.) Nevertheless, I took the news as many of you middle-aged guys would, with no regrets in a lifetime of hunting wild turkeys, upland birds, and waterfowl.

"You may have trouble hearing the voices of women and children," the doctor said seriously.

"How much extra do I owe you for that?" I joked.

Kidding aside, I can still hear turkeys fairly well, but the asymmetrical nature of the hearing loss sometimes makes pinpointing their exact location difficult. To hunt well though, you need to recoup losses. Consider using some of the technical aids on the market, especially during the active-listening part of the hunt. If you're a wingshooter or waterfowler when not turkey hunting and habitually take a lot of shots, wear protective earplugs or other hearing protection. Turkey hunting is a game of listening well, and you can't do it as effectively with appreciable hearing loss.

If a gobble is the most easily recognizable sound in the turkey

As you ease through the woods and along field edges, try to distinguish all the many noises. When you hear something that sounds like a cluck, stop. Listen. It may be a wild turkey asking for you to respond with a turkey call . . .
NATIONAL WILD TURKEY FEDERATION

woods, the cluck is a subtle call you might unintentionally miss. As you ease through the woods and along field edges, try to distinguish all the many noises. When you hear something that sounds like a cluck, stop. Listen. It may be a wild turkey asking for you to respond with a turkey call . . .

There is no strategy quite as satisfying as calling a turkey into range. After all, you've successfully spoken turkey as a second language and fooled a real gobbler or hen into thinking you're one too. Here, Turkey Trot Acres' Pete Clare calls in a New York state fall turkey for his son Drew.

PART 3

Turkey Calling How-To

5

Using Friction Calls

To call wild turkeys effectively you have to know what kinds of calls are out there, and we've covered that. To make those calls you have to understand the language of wild turkeys, and we've addressed that subject too. But it's just a beginning. To render turkey vocalizations you have to know the mechanics of using those calls to imitate turkey vocalizations. Once we've addressed this subject, getting out there to listen to and hunt real turkeys will truly seal the deal. Some of us who have chased them for decades are still learning. There is no strategy quite as satisfying as calling a bird into range. After all, by doing so you've successfully spoken turkey as a second language, and fooled a real gobbler or hen into thinking you're one of them.

In the hands of beginners and veterans, a turkey call is merely a tool full of potential. A friction or mouth call allows you to talk to your wild quarry, but only if you think like the bird you're hunting. Excessive hunter movement and ill-timed calling, failing to acknowledge the bird's keen eyesight, and not understanding that you are speaking a language, can make a turkey go silent. If the scene is repeated on consecutive days, gobblers and hens can feel the pressure and steer clear of you, for no birds are warier than wild turkeys.

Some hunters hold the notion that simply clucking and softly yelping every fifteen minutes is the only way to go. Sometimes, though, aggressive calling is in order, especially when it mimics an excited bird approaching your position. Then again, sometimes only a cluck or soft yelp is called for. In truth, turkey calling—whether you do it in spring, fall, or winter—is an interactive tactic.

How do you actually imitate the diverse turkey vocabulary? What call do you pull from your vest at specific moments during the hunt? When do you make these vocalizations?

FRICTION CALLS

These wild turkey calls require hand movements to create friction between specific calling device surfaces. Different turkey vocalizations

58

result depending on how these calls are held and moved. Hunters often use friction calls to both locate turkeys and initiate a conversation with unseen but vocal birds to draw them into range.

Pot-and-peg, box calls, and push-pull (or push-pin) devices are the most common friction calls. There are a variety of friction calls, including such devices as scratch boxes and the so-called boat paddle. They're generally easy to pick up and use—a plus for the beginning turkey caller and veteran alike.

THE LEARNING CURVE

The corncob-handled ash striker, cheap white string, a palm-sized gray piece of slate, and a boatload of hope didn't call in wild turkeys at first, but it gave me my start. My dad had put that call in my hands, as much an offering toward a potential rite of passage as anything. Maybe he didn't want it. Maybe he was just giving it to me to fool around with. Little did he know what an obsession that calling tool would start.

Our first gobbler hunt that Pennsylvania spring long ago involved a dose of ridge-top silence, at least as gobbling goes, and the memory of sudden movement up the hillside game trail—deer, bear, maybe wild turkey? Red fox. It stopped, frozen in place, not knowing we were silently watching. That animal curled up in the trail like a dog taking a nap. No turkey. Not just yet . . .

I was twelve. It was my first lesson in wild turkey calling: these tools don't always work to lure them in. Okay, maybe they do in some of those television shows that edit out all the effort and waiting. But in reality you'll spend a lot of thoughtful time in the woods and fields attempting to talk turkey. You'll experience frustration, jubilation, false starts, and pure joy at connecting with a vocal bird and pulling it into range with your vocalizations.

The second lesson in turkey calling, again with that crude friction call, came years

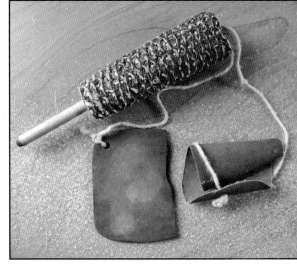

The author's first turkey call, given to him by his father in the 1970s, includes a slate surface, corncob striker, and sandpaper for dressing the slate.

later in college: same developing turkey hunter, still maybe half believing it could be done. I was twenty-one. I stroked out some yelps on that slate call as the misty early morning hillside grew brighter with the oncoming day. I had a single-shot 12-gauge shotgun I'd purchased on my own—but I was still pretty much a novice in the art of running a friction call.

I heard a far-off gobble. A chill of excitement shot up my spine, drilled into the back of my neck, though part of me didn't believe it. I called again to check: silence. What had I done wrong? Nothing. At all.

I now know, after years of calling turkeys with calm and steady confidence based on previous hunts—knowing they may or may not come depending on many factors—that the responsive turkey gobbler may have been on its way that morning before my college classes. Maybe it was just a so-called courtesy gobble, an effort to draw a hen to the male turkey.

I waited, grew impatient, and wanted more. I didn't know how long to wait. While I called again and again, the turkey did not answer. I met my hunting buddy on the trail, and told him about the gobble. "That's really cool, man," he enthused, "I think I heard it too."

Suddenly quick chaos just overhead; wingbeats and sticks breaking off branches: not one but two red-headed jakes flew right out of the trail-

To yelp on a pot-and-peg call like this slate, draw lines or small ovals on the pot's surface. Less pressure makes softer yelps. NATIONAL WILD TURKEY FEDERATION

side pine tree, not high enough to have been roosting (of which I'm now reasonably sure on reflection, especially that far into the morning), but low enough to suggest maybe they hopped up there on our approach. We both got off snap shots. Bang, bang—unanswered prayers for sure. We both cursed, then laughed at the bad luck.

Had I called those turkeys in? Maybe. But it was enough to believe in that crude friction caller. The lesson: gobblers can answer, then come in silently.

USING A POT-AND-PEG CALL

You can make many sounds with that friction call in your hands.

- To cluck, put the peg's tip on the striking surface, angle it slightly inward with pressure, and pull it toward you. Keep that tip on the pot. Soft clucks can be made with less pressure; hard clucks when you apply more.
- To yelp, draw lines or small ovals on the pot's surface. Less pressure makes softer yelps.
- To cutt, make clucks in fast repetitions by keeping the peg's tip on the surface.
- To cackle, mix yelps, then clucks, then yelps.
- To purr, draw a slow line across the pot's surface. Make these lines in an agitated way to imitate fighting birds, while also adding clucks and cutts at the end of those purrs. Turkeys are often drawn to these intra- and inter-flock squabbles.

To yelp, draw oval-shaped patterns on the pot-and-peg call's surface.

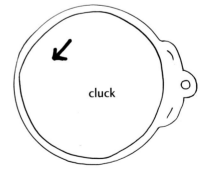

To cluck, apply pressure to the striker, push down and pluck the tip toward you. The peg's tip should skip but touch the surface.

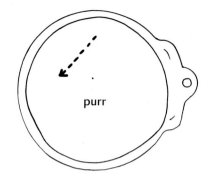

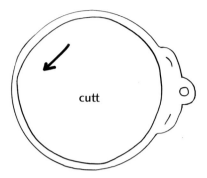

To purr, apply pressure and slowly drag the peg toward you. The striker should skip and drag across the surface.

To cutt, cluck rapidly for six or more times while touching the call's surface. DRAWINGS BY THE AUTHOR

- To *kee-kee*, stroke the peg's tip on the striking surface just inside the call's outside rim to create the three-note sound of a young turkey. Add a yelp or two at the end to make the *kee-kee-run*. Glass surfaces tend to work best.

A pot-and-peg call can make the range of turkey vocalizations during a hunt. Here a hunter calls to a bird in hopes of pulling it closer to his setup. NATIONAL WILD TURKEY FEDERATION

Follow the manufacturer directions provided with your friction call as a starting point, though all hunters have their own particular styles for making turkey talk. I have so many pot-and-peg calls around the house that part of the challenge is simply deciding which one(s) to take along, and yes, that original corn-cob-handled ash striker is still among the options, if only in symbolic memory.

USING A BOX CALL

By the 1940s, Alabama callmaker M. L. Lynch began to market his now-famous box calls to interested parties. On a personal level, my turkey-hunting father purchased one in the mid-1950s at the downtown Emporium, Pennsylvania, gas station where the road-tripping Lynch sold box calls out of his pickup truck.

Rich with personal meaning and turkey-hunting history, that box call (one of the last of the Lynch decorated versions) sits nearby behind glass as I type this. It's interesting to note that in Lynch's time, turkey hunting was only permitted in fifteen states, as opposed to a generous forty-nine now in the spring, and forty-four states in the fall and/or winter.

Striking surfaces must be roughed up (or dressed) to call well. Sandpaper or fine-grit drywall paper works on glass surfaces, while some callers use Scotch Brite scour pads on their slates. NATIONAL WILD TURKEY FEDERATION

Calling devices are now acceptable everywhere wild turkeys are hunted: spring, fall, and winter. In fact, a blended combination of calling tactics and savvy woodsmanship is now considered to be the modern sporting way to take a wild turkey. It took a while, but we got it right.

There are many pot-and-peg call variations, such as these four recent examples from Knight & Hale Game Calls. Striking surfaces vary, and offer a range of possible turkey vocalizations. KNIGHT & HALE GAME CALLS

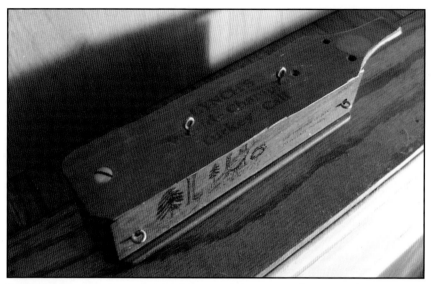

By the 1940s, Alabama callmaker M. L. Lynch began traveling to market his now-famous box calls. The author's turkey-hunting father purchased this one in the mid 1950s at the downtown Emporium, Pennsylvania, gas station where the road-tripping Lynch sold box calls out of his pickup truck.

You'll need a good turkey vest to carry that box call and accessories.

Beyond its rich history, the box call remains an important tool, even in modern turkey vests. I used one as recently as an April 2008 turkey hunt in Texas. Here's how to make the most of yours:

- To cluck on a box call, pop the paddle off the call's lip with short upward strokes.
- To yelp, cradle the box, and lightly scrape and stroke the paddle across the lip.
- To cutt, make a dozen or more fast clucks with sharply repeated pops or taps along the lid.
- To cackle, make a few yelps, then strike the paddle against the call's lip before finishing with yelps.

The author took this west Texas Rio Grande longbeard using a variety of friction calls on a spring afternoon hunt.

- To purr, slowly drag the paddle across the lip. Add soft clucks to this purring to blend calls.
- To *kee-kee* or *kee-kee-run*, find the sweet spot on the paddle near the screw end, then make three whistle-like notes against the lid. Add a yelp or two to render the *kee-kee-run*. Not all models afford this option. Boat paddles often work best.
- To gobble, wrap a rubber band around the paddle to hold it in place, grip the box call without touching the lid, and while holding the handle end up, shake it.

By working the paddle's bottom against the box call's side lips, you can make the entire turkey vocabulary. Box calls should be held firmly but gently, either horizontally in your left hand's palm as you work the lid with your right (your left if you're a southpaw), or vertically, with the front handle up high, and the screw end down low. As with all calls, it pays to practice regularly until you can render realistic turkey talk. Each box offers different qualities. Boat paddles or long boxes do too. Don't forget to tune your call with friction-call chalk before and during your hunt, though some modern-day models require no chalking at all. You can also use a waterproof model.

As part of the continuing learning curve that every turkey hunter indulges in, I found turkey tracks and droppings on a little game trail

To yelp, cradle the box and lightly scrape and stroke the paddle across the lip. To cutt, make a dozen or more fast clucks with sharply repeated pops or taps along the box call's lid. To cackle, make a few yelps and strike the paddle against the call's lip before finishing with yelps.

running under a break in the hog-wire fence on the New Hampshire farm where I was hunting. I had that Lynch box my dad had purchased from the man himself. Lessons were coming fast those days: I'd just finished graduate school, and wild turkey populations were just beginning their steep climb thanks to intense restoration management. I hardly slept the night before, got in there early, and set up at the broad maple nearby. I'd have to rely on my woodsmanship or calling or both, as always.

I yelped on the Lynch box, heard a gobble, felt the chill of anticipation, and waited. Time passed, as they say.

I called again, heard the chatter of a red squirrel, and resolved that maybe the bird was on its way. Squirrels seem to broadcast such news in my experience . . .

Sounds came to my left, and I watched out of the corner of my eye as one by one wild turkeys leapt up on the fence's wooden crossbeam and down to my side. Lesson: turkeys will cross a fence—not always, but this time. A gobbler drifted just in front of my Remington 870's muzzle. Too close, turkey fever rising, I whiffed.

"Where's the bird?" my buddy asked, approaching from a distance after my failed shot.

Another lesson would follow: never give up. I'd heard a lot of things, true and untrue, during my early years as a caller and turkey hunter. Myth 1: You can't call turkeys back to where you missed one. Myth 2: If you *do* try to call one back, you shouldn't use the same call. Myth 3: You can't . . . (fill in the blank)

Box calls are slender, rectangular wooden boxes with gently arched sounding-board sides. The paddle (or lid) sits on top, and is usually attached with a spring-wrapped hinge screw on one end. This lid's length extends to form a front handle, which is held when calling. These two examples are the work of Ohio callmaker Marlin Watkins.

Box calls can imitate the entire vocabulary of the wild turkey, and can attract spring longbeards like these three gobbling birds. D. TOBY THOMPSON/NATIONAL WILD TURKEY FEDERATION

I re-chalked the heirloom Lynch box call, and during hunts over the following week in the same location, I started to buy into those false assumptions. I virtually lived at the base of that maple tree, set up there, stroking yelps on that box, and hoping for redemption. By then my buddy had decided to hunt somewhere other than where his obsessive-compulsive friend did.

Fortunately, I finally heard a strong gobble just up the rise when I called on the Lynch box, on the other side of the fence. This time I didn't miss.

I've had many lessons in my development as a turkey hunter since 1971. This is ancient history to some of you younger guys riding the wave of the modern spring-turkey tradition. It's like yesterday to me: the box call in its many forms has always been along for the ride.

USING A PUSH-PULL CALL

I can easily think of numerous occasions, on both spring and fall turkey hunts, when a push-pull call helped me draw a bird into range. Here's how to work yours more effectively:

Push-pull calls, pictured here, require one or two hands to operate, depending on your calling style. Some models even clip to your shotgun's barrel. These calls can offer superb clucks, yelps, and especially purrs.

- To cluck, tap or pop the plunger sharply.
- To yelp, move the plunger with smooth strokes. Some callers push it. Some pull it.
- To cutt, make repeated fast clucks by tapping or popping the plunger. Mix in yelps to imitate an excited turkey.
- To cackle, make a few yelps, then add popping clucks, before mixing in yelps to finish.
- To purr, slowly push or pull the plunger so that the movable striking surface drags and skips across the fixed striker.

Most push-pull calls operate with a long wire that controls plunger tension. The plunger works the movable striking surface across the fixed striker to create turkey sounds. Callers can tweak this device if notes aren't quite right. Some hunters run these calls by gently palming them while working the plunger with the index finger of the same hand, as if pulling a shotgun's

Use all the friction calls available to you to interest gobblers like this longbeard. NATIONAL WILD TURKEY FEDERATION

trigger. I cradle the call in my left hand, while I pinch the plunger between my right hand's thumb and index finger, and softly stroke it up into the box. This latter technique is particularly effective for making sleepy tree calls to roosted spring and autumn turkeys before fly-down time. I also run this call by positioning the plunger's tip on my knee while moving the box up and down to make clucks, yelps, cutts, cackles, and purrs.

Chalking the striking surface regularly maximizes this tool's potential. Recent models require no chalking and are waterproof. Some styles are even designed to attach to your shotgun's barrel.

USING SCRATCH BOXES

A scratch box is smaller than a typical box call, and it has no hinged paddle.

- To cluck, pop the striker off a lip.
- To yelp, drag the striker across a lip.
- To purr, slowly scrape the striker across a lip.
- To carry it, slip it into your shirt pocket.

Sounds easy, right? In some ways it is. But again, common sense says that time in the woods with the turkeys teaches you how to make the most of your calling abilities. By gently holding the scratch box in one hand and the striker in the other, you can send out clucks, yelps, and purrs. Some callers move the striker against a scratch box's lip (like the bigger box call, or boat paddle, it has two lips), while others move the scratch box against the striker's chalked wooden surface. The chamber's empty space between the two lips makes the sound.

6

Using Air-Activated Calls

Unlike friction calls, mouth diaphragms allow hunters to call without hand movements. Such air-activated devices are both inexpensive and easy to carry. Diaphragms are indeed versatile, though such calls are sometimes difficult to master. Other air-activated devices include tube calls, gobbler calls, wing bones, and trumpet calls. Fortunately, there are many choices.

MOUTH DIAPHRAGMS

- To cluck on a mouth diaphragm, say *pock* or *puck* with snapping, beak-like lips. (I'm serious—if you've watched a turkey calling when afield, you know exactly what I mean. Do it when you yelp as well.) Pop and smack your lips to make this one- to three-note sound.
- To yelp, your tongue should work the diaphragm into the roof of your mouth, latex edge(s) facing forward, creating an air seal. Next, put your tongue lightly against the latex. Blow short yelplike notes of air, pronouncing the words "chop," "chirp," "chalk," or even "chick." Some turkey hunters even say "chee-uck" to

The author took this Missouri longbeard with soft clucks and yelps on a diaphragm call.

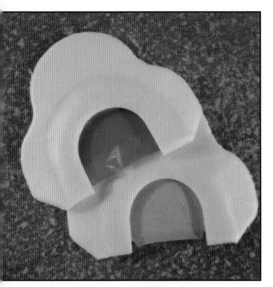

Manufactured diaphragm call options include single, double, triple, notched, split, and stacked reeds. These two Quaker Boy examples are from their "Foam Fit" series.

create the two-note yelp. Many callers drop their jaws during this action. First, make the high end of the yelp. Roll that note into the lower, deeper part of the yelp by letting tongue pressure off the reed. Break the word you are blowing in half. Say *chee*, then *uck*. Do it slowly at first, then blend it together.

You can break the words, "chop" (*ch-op*), "chirp" (*ch-irp*), "chalk" (*ch-alk*), and "chick" (*ch-ick*) in half too as you yelp with the diaphragm. If you are comfortable with a particular mouth call in the spring, it'll suit you fine in the fall and winter for making lost hen yelps, and so forth. Experiment with a variety of diaphragms (and sounds) until you find a style design you prefer.

- To cutt, run clucks together in a fast series, varying the air you blow across the reeds while also snapping your lips.
- To cackle make a rapid *kit-kit-kit-cat-cat-cow* call. This call is a series of fast, excited turkey sounds strung together. It imitates a bird flying off the morning roost, and can pull a turkey in at that time.
- To purr, make a fluttering sound with your throat or tongue, as you expel air across

This Osceola longbeard struts in a Florida pasture. Real turkeys in live situations are the best teachers of all. Scout. Hunt. Hang out with the birds— a lot. BOB LOLLO/NATIONAL WILD TURKEY FEDERATION

the reeds. Turkeys make this call in the wild to space themselves over a food source, and also to indicate a sense of well-being. An agitated purr can also be tagged on the end of a combination of turkey sounds to imitate fighting birds.

- To *kee-kee* or *kee-kee-run*, put a little more tongue pressure on the reed or reeds to get the high note, then keep the sound rising with a kind of lost urgency. Mimic what you're hearing from young birds. To *kee-kee*, say *pee-pee-pee*, and add a couple yelps after that (*chalk-chalk*) for the *kee-kee-run*.

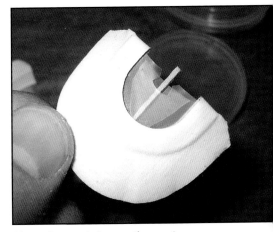

Clean the reeds by gently running a toothpick between them. Be careful not to tear the latex during this process. When storing, place the shortened tip of a toothpick between the reeds so the latex won't stick together when not used.

Mouth diaphragms free our hands to aim that shotgun or bow when the moment of truth arrives, and with a wary wild turkey, you need all the help you can get.
MOSSY OAK/NATIONAL WILD TURKEY FEDERATION

To yelp, your tongue should push the diaphragm into the roof of your mouth, latex edge(s) facing forward, creating an air seal. Next, put your tongue lightly against the latex. Then blow short yelplike notes of air, pronouncing the words, *chop, chirp, chalk,* or *chick.* Some even say *chee-uck* to create the two-note yelp. Some callers drop their jaws during this action.

In my experience, double-reed mouth calls work best for imitating young turkeys. Putting more pressure on the reed makes a higher pitch.

SIX ASPECTS OF MOUTH CALLING TURKEYS

There's more to fooling gobblers with a diaphragm than popping one in your mouth and huffing hot air. Sure, at times an uninspired cluck or several monotonous yelps might drag a spring tom to your setup, but common sense and experience will make you a better caller and a hardcore hunter.

Why choose a diaphragm? Hands-free operation. Realistic sounds. Cost effectiveness. Just ounces to carry, you can hide one in your mouth. Running your mouth call with the right number, rhythm, length, volume, spacing, and pitch of notes will improve your calling game.

1. Count 'Em Out

Listen to enough wild turkeys and you'll hear them consistently call with numerical frequency. The hen's yelp and plain cluck are the two basic vocalizations spring gobbler hunters commonly use. With mouth calling, there's less room for error, so every note counts.

On the roost, a hen's tree yelps range from just one to a handful of notes. On the ground, a hen's plain yelp generally consists of three to five notes, with some situational variation. With more notes, that plain hen yelp becomes an urgent lost call, and might run from twelve to twenty notes or more. A plain cluck is one to three notes, while loud clucking (cutting) includes four to 10 ten notes or more.

Vary the number of yelps and clucks according to the hunting situation. Actively listen to live yelping and clucking hens, then match their calling moment to moment. Be deliberate, not arbitrary.

Are those longbeards henned up? Mimic a vocal hen, call for call,

Once you've become comfortable with a diaphragm call fitted in the roof of your mouth, practice the six aspects of calling turkeys.

using the same number of notes to pull the whole flock—and any gobblers in it—into range. Are those toms silent? Make them sound off with the right number of yelped and clucked notes.

Calling tip: New to this? Try out various mouth calls by making some turkey sounds. Single- and double-reed diaphragms offer stylistic simplicity. Start with plain yelps and clucks. Put the call's horseshoe end on your palate, latex reed(s) facing out. The small bump or tab on most frames should face down. Work the diaphragm into the roof of your mouth with your tongue to get a tight air seal. Root it there or your call won't work. Place your tongue lightly over the reed(s), and huff short yelplike notes of air. Don't blow too hard at first.

Vary the number of yelps and clucks according to hunting situations. Actively listen to live turkeys, and match their calling moment to moment. Be deliberate, not arbitrary. MOSSY OAK/NATIONAL WILD TURKEY FEDERATION

2. Got Rhythm?

Mouth call yelps and clucks should follow a rhythmic pattern. Each hunter has a personal style, but some basics apply.

In the purest sense, a hen's yelps are made with evenly paced beats, while clucks include unevenly mixed notes. Whether that wild turkey is roosted, on the ground, or lost and looking for flockmates, those yelps are steady. In contrast, both the hen's cluck and cutt are notably varied. The rhythm is irregular.

While some mouth callers mix both with success, especially when that spring gobbler is coming on a leash, it's important to note the distinction.

Calling tip: Ask your turkey buds what word they say when yelping, and the answer will likely vary. *Chick, chirp, chop,* and *chalk* are some options, with *ch* as the common sound. Some say *shuck* or *shock* or *shick.* Others say *chee-uck.* Whatever option you choose, call with snapping, beaklike lips, just like a turkey. To practice, choose a single word: *shock.* Break it: *sh-ock.* Then roll it together as you yelp: *s-h-h-h-o-c-k, shhh-ock, shock.* Experiment with these various words to get the sound you want.

3. Note Length

Listen to a yelping hen and you'll notice three or four notes per second in a series: *yawp-yawp-yawp*. A plain *cluck*—*pock*—often fills a brief interval of time. Cutting might include several to a half-dozen notes per second in rapid-fire sequence. Pay attention to note length when you mouth call.

Calling tip: To cluck on a mouth call, say *pock, puck, tock,* or *tuck* with one short burst of air. To cutt, run those clucks together in a fast series: *tuck-tuck-tuck-tuck*. Vary the cadence to imitate live hens you hear when hunting. Mix in clucking and cutting with your yelping.

4. Crank It Up or Tone It Down?

A hen's tree yelping is often faint and muted. It's best heard in range of a turkey roost. If a gobbler is nearby, you may hear his rowdy response. Plain yelping after a hen has flown down is typically nasal in quality. A lost yelp is louder and less subdued. The tonal urgency is easily heard. Practice these variations.

Calling tip: First say each yelp- and cluck-associated word without a diaphragm. Pretty close to a turkey's yelp and cluck, right? That's why some can even talk turkey without a call, using only their voice. Now say these words with your favorite mouth call. Notice how your tongue works to make that sound, and how your jaw drops as you release pressure toward the end of the yelp, and when making the cluck. Not bad, eh? You can adjust calling volume by varying tongue pressure and the air passing across the diaphragm's reed(s).

5. Space It Out

Turkeys looking for each other cluck then often wait one, two, or even three or more seconds before clucking again. This timing distinguishes the plain cluck from cutting.

A plain cluck asks, "Where are you?" when looking for a response from another turkey. In that moment, you can wait silently, and let the bird look for you, or you can answer right back. Space those clucks to mimic the bird that's approaching. Once you call, that turkey has likely fixed your position.

If it's a territorial hen checking you out, look for a spring gobbler bringing up the rear, and key on him. Hen or not, you can cluck hands-free to soft sell an interested tom into slinking into range. This important attention-getting vocalization can be a single note, or several notes.

A cutting turkey will issue a series of abrupt and excited clucks with a second or two of silence before cutting again.

Calling tip: Feeling experimental? Combine diaphragm yelping with pot-and-peg or box-call vocalizations. If it's stormy, the combination helps you call through windy gusts so the gobbler can hear you better. You can also imitate several turkeys this way. Sometimes, that's what it takes.

6. Here's the Pitch

Pitch is the high or low tone within a range of specific calls. A hen's yelp is higher pitched than a gobbler's. Clucks—both plain and those made when cutting—should reflect the same pitch. Contest callers often vary the pitch when cutting on the stage, but if you listen to wild turkeys, chances are you'll hear otherwise.

To begin your spring morning's hunt, make a fly-down cackle with a speedy *kit-kit-kit-cat-cat-cow* call. To purr, flutter your tongue or lips as you expel air across the call's reed(s). Purring can suggest feeding turkeys (call softly) or pecking-order-driven toms ready to fight (add volume). Primarily associated with fall hunting—though I've called in young spring hens that *kee-keed*—a *kee-kee* call can be made by saying *pee-pee-pee*. Tag on several yelps to that series, and you have a *kee-kee-run*. Why use traditional autumn calls in the spring? Some jakes and jennies still make these vocalizations then, and gregarious gobblers sometimes come to most any turkey sound during the breeding season.

Calling tip: Add more mouth calling vocalizations as you progress.

Two adult Merriam's gobblers walk into range. NATIONAL WILD TURKEY FEDERATION

Mouth Call Care

Mouth call care should begin as soon as the call comes out of the package. During the season, and as the season comes to a close, keep your mouth calls in good working order.

Wash mouth calls with warm water to remove any latex residue. Then, if you prefer, soak them in a solution of one part mouthwash, one part water for a few hours before rinsing again.

Pat dry, then store your mouth calls in a plastic case or bag in the refrigerator. This cool, dark environment keeps reeds tight, providing optimum sound. Diaphragm latex can expand, lose pliability, and create too much vibration if not properly stored. Freezing diaphragms works too.

A flat-tipped toothpick, gently run between the reeds to clean them, helps maintain quality. Be careful not to tear the latex during this process. When storing, place the tip of a toothpick between the reeds so they won't stick together when not used.

A well-fitting diaphragm doesn't need tweaking. That good air seal comes immediately. Otherwise, fine-tune your mouth call. If you don't have the right mouth for a standard call, you have to trim your call's frame:

- Using a small scissors, cut the frame's sides first (a little at a time), then the rounded back of the mouth call.
- Don't snip off too much when altering the original.
- Don't trim the latex reeds, only the frame.
- Try the call as you go.
- Once properly sized, make the same cut pattern on your other diaphragm calls to have a consistent frame trim.
- Bend the frame only slightly to adjust it, if you do it at all. Those latex reeds will be affected.

Number, rhythm, length, volume, spacing, pitch: adding all six aspects to your mouth calling repertoire will enhance your game plan this season. In the end, there's nothing more satisfying than speaking turkey as a second language, and fooling a longbeard into range.

Quaker Boy's Ernie Calandrelli runs a tube call during a Missouri spring gobbler hunt.

The author demonstrates proper tube-call placement. In an actual live calling situation, a hand can be cupped around the call to project farther.

USING TUBE CALLS

These small tubes are usually fitted with latex single or double reeds like those on a mouth diaphragm. Once mastered, tube-call yelping can be a great fall locator on calm, windless days. It can entice a silent spring gobbler into revealing its location. The simple call provides loud yelping or rowdy gobbling if needed, but also offers soft close-range clucking. Here's how to use it:

Make turkey sounds by blowing air past the latex and through the tube. Cup your hand or hands around the other end of the call to deaden or project the sound. Manufactured calls vary, so practice is key—calling instructions are often detailed and helpful with each specific industry option. As with cooking wild game recipes, follow the basic steps while improvising a little.

Chances are if you can make the range of turkey calls on a diaphragm, successful tube-call use isn't far behind. However, you may encounter a tickling sensation on your lip when tube calling, or you may have a latex allergy, which like the diaphragm gagging reflex, may push you in the direction of other call choices.

USING GOBBLER CALLS

These air-activated turkey calls contain three sections: the barrel, the sounding chamber, and the weighted bellow. These parts

Gobbler calls can be used just before or after morning fly-down during both the spring and fall seasons, or when a male-only gang of birds is regrouping after an autumn flock bust. LARRY PRICE/NATIONAL WILD TURKEY FEDERATION

create a singular call: the male turkey's gobble. Gobbler calls can be used just before or after morning fly-down during both the spring and fall seasons, or when a male-only gang of birds is regrouping after an autumn flock bust. Gobbles can be tagged on the end of a *kee-kee-run*, as fall jakes will often call. This option is good to have in your spring, fall, and winter calling arsenal.

Here's how to use a gobble call—I emphasize here how to hold it:

- To use just one hand, grip the barrel as if throwing a forkball in a baseball game, with your index and middle finger wrapped around it, and your thumb holding the call in place. Swing your wrist forward and back to produce gobbling.
- Another option is to simply grip the barrel as if holding a glass of water. Swing the call back and forth as if shaking dice.
- You can also simply pump the call quickly—holding the barrel in one hand and moving the weighted bellow up and down in a clean motion with the other.

In the spring, use this call as a locator, as gobblers will sometimes sound off to other male turkeys then. In a common autumn scenario involving young male turkeys, you may make a *kee-kee-run* with a diaphragm before throwing in a gobble at the end.

A Dozen Turkey-Calling Lessons

1. You can use either a primitive call or a modern device to make turkey vocalizations.
2. Confident calling kills many wild turkeys. Overconfidence allows many birds to live another day.
3. Competition callers may win contests but they are not always able to fool gobblers and hens in the wild. Conversely, callers who would never win a sanctioned competition can fool tough wild turkeys.
4. There are some hens and gobblers that would never win a calling contest.
5. You only need one call to fool a wild turkey, but having many more in your vest provides options.
6. You need to find the call that works for *you*.
7. You need to routinely try other calls to confirm your favorite choice, and/or to find another that's better.
8. The (add your favorite call here) is the best turkey-calling tool ever created, but only for someone who knows how to run it.
9. The mouth diaphragm is the most difficult call to use. In the palates of some callers, it sounds exactly like a turkey. In the mouths of others, the sounds might better reflect a barking dog or wailing prey species.
10. So you can't run a mouth call. It's okay. There's a call out there that you can use.
11. The wing-bone call is loaded with personal meaning, especially if made by a friend, family member, or even yourself from the bones of a wild turkey.
12. The box call—like the slate or other pot-and-peg options—is loaded with historical tradition and modern industry innovation. It's the biggest one on the market, and it contains all the turkey sounds you need to make.

A call is only useful if you know what kinds are available to you, know what turkey vocalizations mean, know how to work that call, and even more importantly, know the hunting situations in which to employ a call.

Sometimes you'll still have your doubters. As a guest at a southern turkey camp one spring, I had a discussion with some of the locals who insisted male turkeys don't gobble in the fall and winter. That's news to me. Based on some of my spring hunts there, they don't always gobble then either. In my longtime experience, male turkeys do gobble in fall and winter (though not necessarily as frequently as in spring). Still it's best to get out there yourself to confirm it.

USING WING-BONE AND TRUMPET CALLS

These calls make up in traditional feeling what they lack in versatility. You can cluck with them. You can yelp with them. The best callers I've met can also *kee-kee* and *kee-kee-run* with them. As with the tube call, these tools can locate a silent bird, which might be all you need to bring that bird to your position.

As purist hunting goes, calling in a wild turkey with a tool crafted from the radius and ulna bones of a hen or gobbler the hunter has taken is hard to beat. It connects the hunter with calling history—both personal and traditional. It's simple and basic in an age of excessive complexity.

Modern callmakers have adapted some of the original trumpet-call prototypes, producing their own versions. Others continue to make calls

Writer, editor, wild turkey hunter, and historian Jim Casada runs his wing-bone call during a recent Texas spring gobbler hunt.

Calling with steady confidence tags many spring gobblers. As a hunter and caller, you've got to think like a wild turkey to draw one into range. Overconfidence keeps many birds alive another day.

from the wingbones of turkeys they've taken, preferring these to any store-bought options. Such wind instruments can be effective in spring, autumn and winter. Remember, that's what the Native Americans used as a subsistence tool.

Here's how to begin:

- Practice on wingbone or trumpet calls regularly to make the smack-sucking lip motions necessary to imitate the wild turkey.
- Gently suck air through the call as you hold its far end cupped in your hands.
- Smacking, sucking, and drawing air past your pursed lips can alternately make turkey sounds. The trick is to control your mouth and throat as you make the proper tone and cadence of clucks and yelps.

Final word: Sometimes, I like to mix it up with the many available air-activated calls.

- In an effort to imitate one or more turkeys, I'll yelp on a diaphragm while simultaneously running a friction call.
- I'll finish one series of *kee-kee-runs* while continuing with purrs and cutts.
- I'll empty my vest, and put on a calling clinic.

It's fun when the action is slow and you need to get something going. At times, it even works. Experiment, and try to imagine how you sound to other turkeys nearby. That may be all it takes to draw birds in for a look-see. If you want to be a whole flock, run a bunch of those calls at once.

7

Using Locator Calls

Locator calling for wild turkeys in the spring, fall, or winter includes two basic actions: you make a deliberate sound, then listen for a bird's response. Cold calling to locate wild turkeys is another technique. You can cluck, yelp, and even gobble to find once-silent spring toms. This can also evoke responses from autumn and winter turkeys.

Though underutilized, cold calling to legal but shut-mouthed birds of either sex improves your ability to find fall and winter turkeys. During the woodstove months, you'll locate family flocks, broodless hen groups, and gobbler gangs.

SPRING LOCATOR CALLING

In springtime, hunters focus on hearing that gobble. Other turkey sounds, even those made by hens, can help you locate male turkeys too.

Springtime locator calls are intended to draw a shock gobble from a male turkey. This allows the hunter to know where the gobbler is positioned. Since spring gobblers respond to a range of loud sounds, hunters often use naturally occurring bird vocalizations. The barred owl and crow are the most traditional. Typically, both the barred owl and crow locator calls are shortened so that the hunter can listen for the gobbler's response.

The barred owl's full call goes: *who-cooks-for-you, who-cooks-for-you-all.* A short version might just include one short loud *who-who-whoooah.* After that, listen for the gobble. The difference between locator calling while hunting and owling in a calling competition is marked: one is short; one is more realistic. Then again, if you wish to make the full barred owl call, that can work too.

The common crow's full vocal range is diverse. As with the shortened owl hooting, a *caw-caw-caw* call can draw responses from silent spring gobblers. You don't need to make the entire range of other crow calls.

Traditional wisdom is that it's good to use owl hoots and crow caws when trying to locate a gobbler on the roost, followed by turkey calls once a setup has been established. Other hunters simply locate birds with real

85

Springtime locator calls are intended to draw shock gobbles from male turkeys like these two longbeards. This allows the hunter to know where the gobbler is positioned. Since a spring gobbler responds to a range of loud sounds, hunters often use naturally occurring bird vocalizations. The barred owl and crow are the most traditional. MASLOWSKI/NATIONAL WILD TURKEY FEDERATION

clucks and yelps no matter the time of day, and that can work too. Silent turkeys can walk in on you with the latter approach if you aren't set up. Using owl and crow calls can draw a shock gobble before another calling tactic is employed.

Listening for that gobble after an owl hoot or crow caw is crucial. Don't talk to a buddy right after making the sound. Stay silent. Don't move in place. Hoot. Caw. Listen. If you're with a hunting partner, stand away from the locator caller to hear birds respond.

Eliciting a shock gobble isn't hard. It doesn't always work, but when it does, you know that bird is out there and where it's standing, and that can determine how you will hunt it. If possible, try to let spring gobblers call unprovoked in the half-hour before sunrise and at daybreak while they're still on the roost. If you don't hear anything, then it's time to try the owl hooter and the crow caller.

Eliciting a shock gobble isn't that difficult. It doesn't always work, but when it does, you know that bird is out there and where it's standing, and that can determine how you will hunt it. JOE BLAKE/NATIONAL WILD TURKEY FEDERATION

OTHER SPRING LOCATOR TACTICS

A coyote howler can be one of the best calls to elicit a shock gobble from silent toms. A coyote howl can be as loud or high-pitched as you wish. *Yip-yip-yip-yip-yawwww* is one typical approach. Shorten it as need be. Bark with sharp yaps. Practice with the coyote call to appreciate its full range.

Beyond the owl and crow, try wood duck calls, mallard quacking, and peacock calls, goose calls with just a short honk or two, hawk screamers, pileated woodpecker calls, and even gobbler calls, though with caution. Imitate the great horned owl, which has a softer call: *hoo, hoo-hoo, hoo, hoo*. This species thrives nationwide, and can easily be imitated.

A silent bird might just sound off without your locator calling efforts, so slowly troll along areas where you know gobblers roam. Stop, look, and listen. When locating on public land, stop when you hear that gobbler respond to your locator call the first time. Continuing can risk pulling in another hunter. One tactic is to locate the

A coyote howler and elk bugler first located this Wyoming spring snow longbeard.

Once you locate a spring gobbler, don't continue to use locator calls unless you haven't quite fixed that turkey's position. Reposition if necessary, sit down, set up, and use turkey calls to try to pull that bird into range. NATIONAL WILD TURKEY FEDERATION

evening before your hunt. Note the bird's roosting position. Be there before dawn the next morning.

Listen for other sounds in the woods that might locate the gobbler for you. If a pileated woodpecker sounds off, listen for a gobble to follow. Pay attention to the natural noises around you: blue jays, a branch falling, thunder, geese honking, and so on. All can draw shock gobbles.

Odd sounds can pull a shock gobble out of a bird. What these noises lose in locator calling aesthetics is gained in success. Over the years I've heard of hunters swinging baseball bats against old trees to make a whomping sound before entering the woods. Slammed truck doors can draw shock gobbles, though many of us opt to close them quietly. I once watched as a hunting guide took a large rock and banged it against a guardrail before we headed up the ridge—claimed it got them to shock gobble sometimes. In Wyoming one spring, the *clank-clang* of post-hunt horseshoes hitting a staked steel post caused nearby gobblers in the hills to respond.

Still, sometimes natural sounds are the best way to go. When set up in position, scratching leaves with your free hand can draw a gobble from a radar-eared tom. This works especially well for hard-hunted turkeys near known roosts at fly-down time.

Position matters for locator calling. Get high up on a mountain and listen. Move along slowly at a low-key pace. Use those turkey calls in your vest to pull responses out of quiet gobblers. Don't overdo locator calling. Be selective.

FALL AND WINTER LOCATOR CALLING

A cold, hard northern New England rain fell on October 12, 2007. That was the day before Maine's first modern autumn gun turkey season began. It got me thinking a couple of things: maybe some guys would sleep in, and just maybe the wild turkeys would want to dry off in the morning if the sun came out around flydown time. Sometimes these big birds do that the morning after a

If you've managed to locate a spring gobbler, one option includes staking a decoy to give that turkey a visual reference as it moves toward your position.

This classic Lynch box call can make both high-pitched hen and raspy gobbler yelps for fall hunt locating situations.

steady blow, shaking off in fields like black Labs following water retrieves.

Before the opener I had my occasional pre-hunt breakfast: a hard-boiled egg with a banana for dessert, washed down with hot coffee. Radar, my English setter who knows the difference between camouflage and blue jeans, repeatedly asked—with his gyrating tail and eye-to-eye intensity—if he might go too. We'd done that all week, scratching out a few planted pheasants at the end of his pretty points, hitting our wood-cock covers, and finding none.

I drove slowly through the sleepy neighborhood, hit the red light, waited way too long for the green signal, crossed the main road, and cut through various others, driving until I felt that mix of anticipation (to hunt) and dread (that someone might be there before me). Fortunately I was alone when I arrived. The place had been hit hard by bowhunters since the deer archery season commenced, but maybe they were taking this day off. Too bad—I found whitetails feeding in the field not far from a ladder stand, now unoccupied.

I eased along the field edge, moving slowly as a shadow, noting mallards trading back and forth in the false dawn. It was a pretty morning for sure: the eastern sky was tangerine and pink, swirling with cirrus clouds and rising blue. Gorgeous. A hunting buddy calls October "The Holy Month," and I'm not one to argue.

Molted breast feathers, like this black-tipped feather from a fall gobbler, can alert you to the presence of turkeys.

Still alone. I fully expected company and kept looking over my shoulder for it. This was private land, unposted and open to hunting, and you just don't find enough of that these days. Sunrise, finally, and turkeys, if they were nearby—I'd found a lone molted feather there weeks before—would be flying off their nighttime roosts and down to the ground.

Usually, if you're close enough to roosts in fall, you can hear carrying-on from the bigger flocks: clucking, cutting, yelping, and even gobbling. I heard none of that, but again, I was happy to have the place to myself.

The turkeys would be down on the ground by now. I yelped softly. A turkey yelped back within earshot. I kept easing along the field edge in that direction, moving slowly, full of anticipation, and then I heard it for sure this time: softer turkey talk one field over.

Getting inside the calling zone—the area where a turkey can hear and respond to your clucks, yelps, and other vocalizations—is crucial to hunting success. NATIONAL WILD TURKEY FEDERATION

In the fall woods you can call to get a turkey to answer, or listen for turkeys calling among themselves, or both. After thirty-six hunting seasons I was grateful to still live in a country where I can go out and hunt like this; and after all, wild game is indeed the original organic food.

I focused my attention on listening for the sound of calling, so when I eased forward as slowly as the dark shadows receding, I stopped. Turkeys—a good-sized flock. Now I had to quickly choose from my many calling options, and you don't always have much time in the turkey woods to think. Things change—fast.

I could try to call the whole bunch to me—sometimes one will come and the others will follow, or sometimes one will simply come. Sometimes they never come. I decided to reposition in the woods, moving slowly over the soft wet ground in an effort to put myself in a better calling position. It only took five minutes or so, but seemed like a month as deliberate steps put me where I wanted to be.

Finally, I arrived. I called softly: *yawp-yawp-yawp*. Then a response—followed by a turkey coming, craning its neck, looking for the source of the sound, fifteen or twenty turkeys behind it, still feeding, some looking, and my attention on the one bird.

It was close, too close maybe. One of the new extended-range turkey loads was chambered in my shotgun, a shell that's good for that extra distance when you need it. My friends will tell you I like to let turkeys hunt down my calling position, as that's the thrill of the game. Twenty yards to maybe thirty-five is good for me. This one was around eight steps, and moving closer—so much for using an extended range load. I put the bead on it, and saluted him. Bird down. Game over. That Maine fall turkey graced our Thanksgiving table.

Tree calling to locate the exact location of a fall flock when set up near roosted turkeys can initiate a successful hunt.

All turkeys are meaningful to me, the big toms topping twenty pounds and the fall birds-of-the-year. This one was no exception: an autumn jake, with a full frame and filling out. He weighed in the low double digits. Of the turkey's stubby beard, the New England gentleman at the check-in station remarked: "Well, you've got to sta't somewhere." Indeed. Twice these autumn birds had been silent, and twice I'd located them by cold calling.

TREE CALLING

No, you don't climb a tree to do it. You make these sounds, and listen for them, when turkeys are still on the roost. Since roosted autumn and winter turkey flocks involve adult groups, or family flocks with brood hens and juvenile birds of either sex, the calling you make and encounter before fly-down will differ.

Tree calling involves three primary turkey vocalizations: clucking, yelping, and gobbling. Used to encourage silent tree-bound turkeys to sound off, cold calling can be varied to reveal flock members' exact or probable location.

Roost Clucking (Either Sex)

Turkeys are roosted. You want them to fly down nearby, and come to your calls.

Locator call: Set up where you've roosted fall turkeys, or where you expect flocks might sleep. Make a plain cluck with one to three soft notes. Space it out. Avoid clucking loudly, at least at first. Less is more when trying to locate turkeys just waking up in the morning.

One tree-bound cluck made by turkeys indicates contentment, while the other—often called "pitting" or "putting"—is an urgent, alarm call. The first is a sound made by roosted birds before fly-down to ask, "Where are you? I'm here." The other, the pitting cluck, says, "Predator below. Get ready to flush." You hear it on getting too close to roosted birds.

Ground Clucking (Either Sex)

Turkeys have flown down, assembled, and moved off. You want to find them.

Locator call: Leave several seconds between your clucks when trying to locate unseen birds. Clucks and alarm putts are similar. Both attempt to get another turkey's attention. Cutting is simply a series of loud clucks with an irregular, urgent rhythm, and the same pitch. This can be used to evoke a response from a silent single bird or flock member. The plain cluck is one to three spaced notes.

Roost Yelping (Hens)

Roosted turkeys are waking up, and getting ready to fly down. Your soft yelping to birds on the roost might pull the flock into range when they hit the ground. You are trying to act like one of those turkeys.

Locator call: Cold calling with soft yelps can be made in a location where you've found fresh turkey tracks, scratchings, droppings, or feathers. You need to be close to the roost to hear responses to your locator yelping. Once you cold call with soft hen yelps, listen intently for a turkey to call back. Don't overdo it though, as this call is muted, generally three to five notes long.

Cold call with soft yelps in a location where you've found fresh turkey tracks, scratchings, droppings, or feathers. You need to be close to the roost to hear responses to your locator yelping. Listen intently for a turkey to call back to your vocalizations.

Soft, nasal yelping often begins in the false dawn, or as daylight breaks. Its purpose is to notify flock members of their specific locations before fly-down. Often a brood hen makes this sound in the autumn. Broodless hen groups will communicate this way before fly down too.

GROUND YELPING (HENS)

Make the plain or lost yelp to locate adult or juvenile turkeys while cold calling in the fall.

Locator call: Lost yelping is one way to pull a response from nearby but silent birds. *Kee-kee*ing and *kee-kee-run*ning is another, as it will sometimes evoke an assembly call from the brood hen, which, like the lost yelp, is urgent and many-noted.

A plain yelp has roughly three to nine notes, and is made with less urgency than an assembly or lost yelp. An assembly yelp is made by the brood hen to gather young turkeys after fly-down, or following a flock break. A lost yelp is made by individual adult hen turkeys (or sub-two-year-old hens in their second fall) to indicate they are looking for other birds. Both assembly and lost yelping have more notes (fifteen or twenty isn't unusual) and are louder and often raspier than the typical plain yelp. A hen's yelping is generally higher pitched than a gobbler's.

Lost yelping is one way to pull a response from nearby but silent birds. *Kee-keeing* and *kee-kee-run*ning is another. It will sometimes evoke an assembly call from the brood hen, which, like the lost yelp, is urgent and many-noted.

Roost Yelping (Gobblers)

Use roost yelping to locate silent male birds on the roost, and to evoke responses from these turkeys, revealing their position.

Locator call: Set up near a likely roost site, near where you've noted gobblers the afternoon before, and call as first light arrives. Fall jakes, and so-called super jakes born in the spring or summer of the previous year, sometimes offer raspy, slower two- to three-note yelps on the roost. Juvenile gobblers born that year add a gobble on such calling as well—occasionally a poor barking effort at best. As with roosted hen yelping, these vocalizations are soft and muted.

Ground Yelping (Gobblers)

You know gobblers have roosted nearby and flown down, and you want to find them. Gobbler yelp to get a bird to answer. Or gobbler yelp to evoke a response from a gobbler group you've flushed. Your initial call will often get others talking back.

Locator call: Slate calls are superb at creating raspy gobbler yelps. Many mouth calls tend to be higher-pitched to imitate hens. If you have a diaphragm that is low-pitched, use it to make gobbler yelps. Once on the ground, gobbler yelps can be louder and more intense. As with roost yelping, it includes several notes.

Set up near a likely roost site where you've noted gobblers the afternoon before, and call as first light arrives. Fall jakes and so-called super jakes, born in the spring or summer of the previous year, sometimes offer raspy, slower two- to three-note yelps on the roost and after fly-down. NATIONAL WILD TURKEY FEDERATION

Roost Gobbling

You know where gobblers might roost, and want to pin that location down.

Locator call: Use a gobbler call at daybreak to elicit a response from roosted male turkeys, allowing you to note their position.

While some hunters might argue gobblers don't gobble at all outside of spring, experience shows otherwise. Outside the breeding season, male birds continue to focus on establishing, contesting, and maintaining pecking-order status. They gobble on the autumn roost, not to attract hens, but to vocalize their presence to other male birds.

Ground Gobbling

You want to raise a response from a male bird in the woods, or locate the presence of a gobbler after a flushing situation.

Locator call: Gobble to adult toms in a cold-calling situation, or during a post-flush, call-back session. Add a gobbler call on the end of a *kee-kee-run* to locate juvenile males.

Fall gobblers gobble to each other. Adult longbeards do it after fly-down, and in post-flush situations to regroup.

Starting a Fight

Interested in making silent fall and winter gobblers more vocal? If you've roosted male turkeys that are staying quiet on their limbs, set up nearby before daybreak, then start a fight after fly-down. If you've ever heard a group of male birds in a post-roost rumble, you know that the event is rowdy and loud. Imitate that.

To evoke the kind of a response where gobblers might run to your setup, start out with muted clucking and gobbler yelping while turkeys are still roosted. When you have a sense that fly-down time is nearing, use your hat or other manufactured device to imitate the wingbeats of turkeys clawing through tree branches. This is optional, but some hunters do it.

Then make your gobbler yelping more agitated and your calling more insistent. You can sometimes draw a gang of male birds in for a look using both a mouth call for yelping (avoid high-pitched diaphragms) and a slate call to make urgent yelping and fighting purrs.

Add gobbles to the calling clinic you're offering as well, but always with safety in mind. You can use that hat or wingbeat-making device to imitate gobblers hitting each other as they purr. At any rate, this kind of extreme fall calling should be made only once or twice during the fly-down period as birds move off the roost to the ground. Prolonging the call is unrealistic.

You can also use this fighting approach if you're just entering a pure situation during a hunt, and some time has passed between fly-down and turkeys walking about on the ground. Often gobblers will sound off as they approach. In such situations, I've seen autumn longbeards strut and gobble with anticipation as they draw nearer.

NO-TALK TURKEYS

Turkey calls are fun to use, but at times the birds are quiet. They may rely simply on visual evidence that their flock is nearby. Other times we may call to a once-vocal bird, only to have it go silent. It may be approaching; it may be drifting off. Turkeys are

To locate and call in birds consistently, you need to maintain a level of confidence. You need to use all the available calls.

Trust yourself and your calling abilities. If there's fresh evidence of wild turkeys nearby, hang in there and you might walk out of the woods with a tagged bird.

fairly gregarious, but that doesn't always mean they want to investigate your calling.

Yes, it's true that lost or solitary turkeys will sometimes match you call for call, then come into your setup as if on a long leash. That's gratifying stuff, for sure. Other times, they may show up by walking in silently. Patience is key. They're coming to your calls, just not on your watch.

Fight the urge to fidget while waiting on birds. To learn this, you may need to experience the awful feeling of standing up, perhaps persecuted by rain, biting bugs, or gusty wind, only to have a silent wild turkey flush nearby. You didn't hear it so you thought it wasn't there. Yes, you called that bird in. Yes, the game might be over—for now. Yes, you might be able to locate that turkey once more, and call it back if you reposition. Maybe other flock members are regrouping, so just sit tight. Relax. Trust yourself. If there's fresh sign of turkeys, hang in there.

WALK LIKE A TURKEY

Want to know one of the best ways to locate turkeys? Walk like one. I'm serious. Ever try moving slowly through the woods, occasionally scuffing the leaves with your boots? This imitates a feeding or approaching bird.

Unseen gobblers on the prowl might sound off if they're within earshot. Your walking in the leaves might sound like a hen approaching a gobbler. Remember, a spring gobbler gobbles to encourage hens to do that too. Try to walk naturally. Don't stumble over rocks or break sticks as you approach that bird. Study the ground. Move like smoke. Fall turkeys might cluck at you as you ease through the woods too.

SCRATCHING LEAVES

This approach can draw the same gobbling response from a male bird, but instead you're seated and stationary. If you're hunting a known turkey location and you're not getting a response from vocal birds, or you had a turkey coming to your calls but it hung up, don't call. Scratch leaves instead. Sometimes it works.

The ideal calling setup is a broad-trunked tree with available shooting lanes.

PART

4

When, Where, and Why

8

Situational Calling Strategies

Once you've located some wild turkeys, your ability to call them effectively can depend on your woodsmanship. No matter how talented you are at making turkey vocalizations, how you position yourself for the morning's hunt can dramatically affect your ability to pull a bird into range.

If you're a veteran turkey hunter, you're nodding your head. If you're just starting out, you're all ears. I relearn these lessons myself every season, spring and fall.

After you've located a spring gobbler you've got to analyze the terrain. You've got to figure out the many options for hunting fall and winter

Challenging setups, like this one in Wyoming, involve picking the best spot based on what the terrain has to offer. You'll plunk your seat cushion down at the base of that hardwood, softwood, fencepost, brushy cover, or almost nothing at all if your call-carrying turkey vest provides that kind of support.

flocks. After breaking up a group of autumn turkeys—an effort to separate gregarious birds before attempting to call them back—you need to sit down in a spot that will put you in a good position to call your quarry in and take it.

The ideal calling setup is a broad-trunked tree with available shooting lanes. You'll plunk your seat cushion down at the base of that hardwood, softwood, fencepost, or nothing at all if your vest provides that kind of support (some do). Ideally you'll be in a place where you can pull the trigger on a turkey you've called in. It's always best to get as close as you can without spooking birds, and before attempting to call a turkey.

ROOST SITE SETUPS

You may need to get in tight to close the deal. Take, for example, the morning setup on a roosted spring gobbler.

First of all, you need to throw out that playbook that says setting up over a football field away on a roosted gobbler is the way to go. Yes, sometimes that works, especially on pressured birds. The trick to toppling some tough longbeards is to sneak in early, and set up close, well before sunrise. You may need to use extreme tactics. Sometimes you have to toss out timeworn tradition to legally take dogwood-time turkeys.

You can get close to that bird another way—by watching it fly up as darkness falls. It's one thing to locate spring turkeys from mountain roads at daybreak. It's another to watch them fly to the roost the day before. If you have nailed the exact location of turkeys the afternoon before, you can approach that roost under the cover of night, well before

Getting close to the roost with your morning setup can close the deal on fall turkeys, like this New York state jake that came to the author's calling.

At morning fly-down, spring gobblers sometimes enter fields at the highest point of open pastures, often following hens that take them there. In this situation, your morning setup before fly-down time should be between the nearby roost and high-point strut zone, but still inside concealing edge cover, with shooting lanes in front of you. John Hafner, photographer and turkey hunter, tagged this fine Wyoming longbeard as the strutting bird and hens moved to higher ground.

sunrise. You can be there when they wake up.

After roosting a gobbler, hunt that bird seriously. Sure, spring turkey camp is plenty of fun, especially if you're hunting with buddies, but pace yourself until after you tag your bird. Get up an hour earlier than you typically would and quietly establish your setup in the dark. That'll put you in a position to hunt a roosted gobbler at fly-down time. Don't squander the opportunity. Finish the job.

Hands-free mouth diaphragms are the best choice for tight setups where the turkeys might see the hand movement required for friction calls.

Are your turkeys regrouping after fly-down and not coming in? Are they hanging close, but still out of range? Try plan B: the fall hunting technique of flushing flocks. Flushing roosted flocks after fly-down (or while still on the roost), especially when you separate hens from the dominant gobbler, can provide fast and furious action as that lonely longbeard seeks out scattered hens.

Extreme roost setups should be part of your repertoire. You have to know when to force the issue. I once scouted a New Hampshire spring gobbler before the season on an unposted farm that routinely saw in-season hunter traffic. Not only would killing the bird prove challenging, but I'd have to consider Opening Day influences. So, I did a number of obsessive-compulsive things all of us die-hards favor. I roosted the turkey on a regular basis in the weeks before the Opener, using locator calls. Sometimes he favored one side of the river; sometimes my side on the farm. The late afternoon before the Opener I was fortunate to locate the tom on my side, so I sat down in the woods, and waited for him to fly up. Another scouting hunter walked right past me. By the way he was moving I could tell he was late for something. That worried me a little, but I'd just have to play my hand.

The next morning I parked my truck well before dawn and walked the half mile to the bird. I found the tree I'd picked the day before and slunk down, mouth diaphragm tucked in my cheek. The bird first gobbled on the roost—on a limb, but well under 100 yards from my position. I stayed quiet, but I heard a far-off hunter romance his barred-owl hooter.

Big wings ticked branches on the way to the ground. Once there, the turkey gobbled some more. That's when I first called. He ripped back on the edge of range—unseen through ground cover. I held the assumed shooting position, mentally willing the bird into range, my shotgun affixed to my bent left knee. Unfortunately, the turkey hung up. I called, eager to close the deal. He'd have no part of it. Were other hunters listening to my tomfoolery? Were they moving in on the vocal gobbler? Such are the thoughts of a turkey-obsessed hunter.

So I shut up. So did the bird, fortunately. I waited a long time, sensing the gobbler was in no hurry. Clearly I needed another approach to

Know the terrain in order to establish the best calling setups. NATIONAL WILD TURKEY FEDERATION

Some gobblers roost above water, which likely offers a sense of security. They fly down to dry areas inside the swamp or river bottom, and move to open fields. This Florida turkey hunter has established a calling setup with a clear view of the action. NATIONAL WILD TURKEY FEDERATION

unhinge the bird, so I spit out the mouth diaphragm. I called softly with my natural voice: *yawp-yawp-yawp*. *Grrobble* came the response after many long minutes of shared silence. The tom was right there, right now, well within range. He'd waited all that time.

The gobbler leaned forward, almost imperceptibly. That was the last thing that longbeard saw. Getting tight and knowing that turkey well had worked this time.

Where you set up and attempt to call in a gobbler can make all the difference. You've got to envision what that roosted tom will do at fly-down time and immediately after. At morning fly-down, spring gobblers sometimes enter fields at the highest point of open pastures, often following hens that take them there. In this situation, your morning setup before fly-down time should be between the nearby roost and high-point strut zone, but still inside concealing edge cover, with shooting lanes in front of you. Sit. Wait. React.

Swamp gobblers—Osceolas and even Easterns, for instance—often roost above water, which likely offers a sense of security. They fly down to dry areas inside that swamp, and move to open fields. Put your setup somewhere along the dry-land travel lane between the swamp roost trees and the strut zone. Hub-style camo blinds may help you sit tight.

Some spring gobblers roost in wooded cover, then fly down into forested lanes and tree lines between fields as they move. Rio Grande gobblers and Merriam's turkeys, challenged by wide-open surroundings, seem to prefer this concealed mode of travel. Place your setup inside that cover, along their fly-down landing strip. (Tote a penlight to spot snakes and prickly-pear cactus down south before you sit on your cushion in the dark.) Turkey movement along travel lanes right after fly-down should allow you to call to birds as they ease along inside field cover.

You'll need to rise early to get above mountain gobblers. Got turkeys roosted on the hillside? Place yourself on the plateau above them—close but unseen. At daybreak, or after fly-down, initiate a conversation with the birds and try to pull one directly into your setup.

Maybe you've set up in one place, and the turkeys fly down and drift the other way. The next morning you set up there, and birds fly down and go where you were the day before. Solution: put a buddy in one location, while you claim the other. Double-teaming fills tags too. As always, it pays to think like a turkey.

No luck after morning fly-down? Return to the location later that afternoon if all-day hunting is available. The author took this Texas longbeard by first locating it with a friction call about a quarter mile from where it had roosted that morning. He then eased in closer to the gobbling turkey, picked a setup, and called it in.

THEIR LAND, EVERYBODY'S TURKEYS

Ever notice how often state land flanks posted private property? I've seen this almost everywhere I've hunted around the country. It's like the line has been drawn in the sand, and you can't cross it. Let's say a spring gobbler sounds off on posted land, but definitely in calling range, while you stand on property where you have permission to hunt. Do you:

    A. Push the envelope a little, and cross onto posted land to call the bird, knowing it's unlikely you'll get caught?

    B. Set up on the property where you have permission, and attempt to call that gobbler off posted land, and into range?

    C. Walk away and find another gobbler that wants to play on the property where you have permission to hunt?

If possible, always ask a landowner for permission to hunt turkeys on his land. Still, if you have permission on an adjacent property, there's nothing illegal or unethical about calling a turkey to your setup there.
NATIONAL WILD TURKEY FEDERATION

If your yelping manages to pull a longbeard through an opening in a hogwire fence to your position, congratulations are in order. Anyone who tells you differently hasn't hunted enough turkeys in this age of fragmented habitats.

Sure enough, landowners have every right to prohibit you from hunting their property. You wish it were otherwise, but that's a modern-day hunting reality. Setting one foot on their land is flat-out against the law, and not playing the game by the rules. As a result, answering "A" should be ruled out by every turkey hunter reading this. Don't do it.

True, the person who nailed posted signs to trees likely holds the deed to the land. They don't own the turkeys that live there though. That public resource belongs to everyone, especially hunters who buy licenses and fund wildlife management efforts around our nation. Based on this thinking, "B" is a perfectly legitimate move. It's impossible to trespass on land on which you don't set foot. Period. Calling turkeys off someone else's land is perfectly legal.

Calling posted birds off someone else's property isn't an ethical issue at all. If your yelping manages to pull a longbeard through an opening in a hogwire fence to your position, congratulations are in order. Anyone who tells you differently hasn't hunted enough turkeys in this age of fragmented habitats.

While "C" won't put that gobbler in your vest, sometimes that's an option too. As a sportsman, you may simply cut that tom some slack. Maybe that turkey will be cruising on the unposted land you hunt the next day, or later in the season.

I'll be the first to tell you that you have to play the game legally in order to take satisfaction in tagging a spring gobbler. That's a given. Setting foot on someone else's property violates the sporting ethic. Not only that, it can lead to license revocation and a loss of privileges. Calling turkeys to your setup on land you have permission to hunt is an entirely different matter.

To call turkeys from one posted location to one you can hunt, you need to read the land. You not only need to know your limitations, but also your range. Here are some situations, and possible responses to these challenges:

If a stream or creek divides posted and unposted property, try to find a spot on the side of that waterway that is within the lawful boundary. Call the turkey to that location.

- If a stream or creek divides posted and unposted property, try to find a spot on the side of that waterway that is within the lawful boundary. Call the turkey to that location.
- If a dirt road or trail divides posted and unposted property, set up on the legal side, and call the bird to that spot. Hot gobblers often take the path of least resistance (i.e., a road or path) and move right into your range.
- If heavy cover falls between that gobbler on posted land and your position where permission has been granted, find an open lane on either side of that thicket. When the bird struts in for a look on your side of the line, take him.
- If the gobbler is loudmouthed but hung up on posted property, keep moving around the periphery of the posters, calling on quick

The sign says it all.

setups to take his pulse. He may think you're a hen on the move—possibly going away from him. Use caution, though. If he can see your general position, he may just pop into strut, knowing you (the hen) should see him too. Find a way to set up just inside a concealing canopy. That way he may wander even closer, and into range on unposted land.

- If the gobbler roosts on unposted land but flies down to posted property, get in there early and set up close to the roost. Stake a bunch of decoys in the dark, slip a mouth call into the roof of your mouth, and wait. When he starts sounding off, offer some soft clucks and yelps. Don't overdo it, and definitely don't move. That tom may fly right down into your lap.

You may have to call gobblers off posted property from fairly long distances. You have to hear them first, though. If you have hearing difficulties, consider purchasing a high-tech listening device to pinpoint far-off toms before you try to call them onto legal land.

You need to consider the call too. If you typically use just one turkey call, consider using many at your setup. That might just spark a gobbler's curiosity so that he steps in for a look, crossing onto your unposted side of the fence.

If there is a fence separating the two properties, find a break in the barrier through which turkeys might move. Droppings, feathers, and tracks indicate regular use in these travel ways. Set up nearby.

Take along calls that project great distances. Boat paddles and mouth calls are good choices. You can even run both at the same time to really reach out and touch toms on posted properties. If you raise a turkey that's far off, stick with it as long as it seems to be moving closer, or if it's gone silent. If it seems hung up and you can't approach it due to property lines or terrain, try taking a nap. That may give you the patience to let that bird move closer—on turkey time.

Those calls in your vest—old ones and new models—are capable of calling a gobbler from posted land to your fixed position on land where you have permission to hunt.

WHEN IT WORKS

I was 500 miles from home and on the lookout for New York state public hunting land. Suddenly I noticed a pretty piece of farmland, and a steep slope nearby that likely held roost trees. I pulled off the road, and studied the maps strewn all over my truck's passenger seat. My finger traced the steep slope up, then over to . . . what the—a Wildlife Management Area? I knew one was nearby, but I had no idea it was this close. I thoroughly studied the map and parked my rig.

The beauty of state land is that property lines are clearly marked with signs—no guesswork necessary. After surveying the area, I decided to climb a power line on the WMA's steep sidehill. It took me over an hour to reach the top, and with a little over an hour to go until noon (when shooting hours ended), I cold called. A gobbler answered down the hillside, still on posted land. I could barely hear the bird, but it surely had heard me.

I plunked a decoy down on legal land, a rare thing in itself since I hardly ever use fakes, and I set up. I yelped simultaneously with a push-pin call in one hand and a diaphragm in the roof of my mouth. The tom barked back, clearly closing the distance. At that, I shut up, my shotgun facing the decoy.

It can be done. The author took this self-timer image after he successfully called this 21-pound New York state tom off posted private land to legal public property. The spring gobbler, tagged in May 1996, had inch-plus spurs, and a dragging beard.

I heard footsteps in the leaves to my left (west), either another hunter moving in on me, or that late-morning gobbler. Luck was on my side. The tom cruised by at no less than ten steps, and eased toward that foam fake like a ghost. I clucked. His head periscoped up, and I took him.

I had located that tom on posted land, but dropped him on public property. His weight (21 lbs. and change), 1-inch-plus spurs, and a dragging beard told me he'd been around a long time.

CALLING TACTICS

Those calls in your vest can lure a gobbler to your fixed position from posted land, but some variation to the usual approach might be in order.

Cutting will surely work to locate silent toms, but that doesn't always mean the turkey will come to you. You might need to switch to other calls to lure that gobbler the entire distance. Lost hen yelping can both locate and attract spring gobblers in posted/public situations. Loud by nature, this call involves a long string of yelps that rises in intensity and volume before fading. You can make a racket and still sound natural this way. Fifteen to even twice as many notes aren't out of the question.

Sometimes you need every call in your vest to lure turkeys to your position. Cutt. Yelp. Cackle. Rest a bit. Cluck. *Kee-kee.* Put on a calling clinic. The gobbler may not come the whole way, but he may come just a little bit closer. Try alternating silence with heavy doses of calling. This is a great approach during the mid-morning lulls in the spring turkey woods.

Remember the questions I asked at the start of this section? Let's add a fourth option—D: Ask permission to hunt the posted land. The worst the landowner in question can say is, "No." Places I hunt are often a patchwork of public and private properties, and I'm sure it's like that for you too. Spring gobblers don't know this of course, and roam widely, seeking out hens to breed. Birds that have wandered onto private land can be hunted if you can get permission. And they can always be called off posted land if you can't.

WEATHER AND TURKEY CALLING

You can't kill a gobbler while watching the Weather Channel back at camp—you've got to get out there. True enough, cold weather will sometimes shut down turkey talk, but you've got to persevere to find that longbeard that's ready to wear a tag with your name on it. Here are ways to fight the weather and improve your calling efforts:

1. You can't beat the weather if your clothing doesn't fight the elements. Dress to fit the part. Layer yourself.

2. Yes, keep an eye on the Weather Channel, check online radar tracking, and even use some of your own amateur forecaster's common sense; then hit those windows of opportunity between spates of rain and spring snow. Wild turkeys actively respond to such calm, sunny or precipitation-free shifts in weather too.

3. Windy night? Chances are turkey flocks are treed in protected draws, away from the stiff breeze. Calm evening?

You can't kill a gobbler while watching the Weather Channel back at camp. You've got to get out there. Cold weather will sometimes shut down turkey talk, but you've got to persevere to find that longbeard that's ready to wear a tag with your name on it.

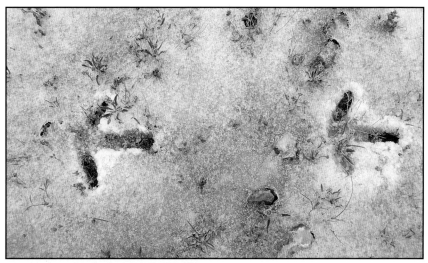

Follow fresh turkey tracks during springtime snows the same way you would follow an autumn whitetail or elk during early winter snows. This can put you in position to use locator, mouth, and friction calls. The author took this photo during an April snow event on a west Texas spring turkey hunt.

Birds are likely less concerned about sheltering cover. Sometimes turkeys sleep on limbs above rivers and swamps in areas where such habitats afford protective cover.

4. On rainy, windy days, strutters and hens often gravitate to open fields. Are open-area food sources nearby? Hens will hit them, and longbeards will follow. Be there.

5. Use the classic crow and owl locator calls, but try others in specific geographical regions, such as elk buglers out west (though it's a fall call, you're now using it in the spring to find gobblers) or coyote howlers almost anywhere.

6. Follow fresh turkey tracks during springtime snows the same way you would track a whitetail or elk. This can put you in position to use locator, mouth, and friction calls. I've recently done so successfully in both Texas and Wyoming in the spring. In fall and winter, track flocks to their location before applying hunting tactics.

7. In the good old days, we turkey hunters used to put our friction calls in plastic bags to keep moisture out. Now you can use the waterproof calls.

8. Don't be timid. Once you get those reluctant cold-weather birds to sound off to your locator calls, bring them in with a series of aggressive yelps and cutting.

BODY LANGUAGE AND TURKEY CALLING

Reading a spring gobbler's body language, and studying how that bird approaches your calling position—or not—can provide a few rules and options of engagement for next season, and maybe even yield a bird by the feet. Relax, sit back, and open your playbook to page one.

What should you do if a turkey gobbles while walking away? What if he gobbles every five minutes or so, but won't budge? What if he flicks his wings, and turns to leave? There's a response for every turkey move.

Body Language—The Walk Away

If a spring turkey gobbles while walking away, he's indicating that initial interest in your calls is passing. He may have wanted that hen to walk up to his position, but since you're a human hunter imitating a female turkey, you obviously didn't. Your response to that tom's departure:

What should you do if a turkey gobbles while walking away from your setup? What if he gobbles every five minutes or so, but won't budge like this Merriam's longbeard? What if he flicks his wings, and turns to leave? There's a calling response for every wild turkey move.

BOB LOLLO/NATIONAL WILD TURKEY FEDERATION

- You might just sit tight and let that bird drift off.
- You might quietly reposition ahead of that gobbler, trying to anticipate where you can set up to call him in again.
- You might just switch calls, or add even more excitement to your calling effort.

He's still there. You can try to call him later on that day, if legal, or later that week, if time provides. Or you might just decide that the hunt was fun, and leave it at that.

If a stone wall is in the way, a turkey may not cross it at first, but repeated calling efforts might convince the bird to fly-hop up there and walk in. Or you can simply reposition to call that turkey into range. NATIONAL WILD TURKEY FEDERATION

Body Language—Walk This Way

Analyze the terrain to make sure it's not stifling a gobbler's efforts to move toward you. Is there a wall, creek, or fence in the way? Is there brush that the turkey doesn't want to enter? Is that tom in heavy cover, and acting like it doesn't want to leave? To get that bird to walk your way you might have to do a number of things:

- You can set up below or above the gobbler based on an imagined line it might walk toward you.
- You can advance, slipping forward five or ten steps if foliage provides cover. If you can see the turkey strutting, move when its fan is turned toward you and its head is hidden from view. Don't stalk. Reposition.
- If a stone wall is in the way—not uncommon here in New England—the bird may not want to cross it at first, but repeated calling efforts might convince it to fly-hop up there and walk in.

- If a creek flows between you and the gobbling tom, get on the other side, and anticipate how it might walk in to you.
- If a fence is in the way, establish your setup so the turkey might go under the obstruction, as holes in such farmland structures are common. Maybe, as with the creek, you'll have to get on the other side to have that tom walk to you.

Body Language—Cement Feet

This spring gobbler has staked out his strutting zone, vocalized his presence, and is asking for you (the hen imitator extraordinaire) to walk to him. He won't budge. Been there? What are your options?

You can have a buddy slowly walk in a straight line away from your original setup while you stay put. Once he's established a new position, he can call. Study the woods for a sign that the turkey is moving toward where it last heard hen yelping, where you still sit silent.

You can also treat the stalemate as simply "locating" a bird, and return there the next morning. Establish your setup near that strut zone.

Body Language—Wing Flick and Turn

Uh-oh. The gobbler has decided to come to you, but the shot it presented wasn't the best. Now the bird has decided the hen he heard isn't there, and that's unusual. The wing flick and turn, a kind of turkey pirouette, is a sure sign he's outta there.

If he's in range—within that distance your shotgun, your choke tube, and the payload has proven suitable before—shoot him in the back of the head and neck. (A turkey doesn't need to be facing you for a shot, but still aim for the head and neck.) If he's not in range, let him drift out of view, then call to get him to gobble so you can fix his location. Reposition a slight distance away, and call him back in.

If he's really walking away fast, let him go. Relax. Pour yourself a cup of coffee. Eat a snack. Strategize, or just go find a fresh bird.

Toms that gobble at your calling but don't come may have dominance issues. They may not want to go into an area for fear a boss gobbler will fight them off. Its attempt to call that hen out of your location has less to do with your abilities than natural order.

Body Language—Dialing Long-Distance

Have you located a spring gobbler that's far off, but coming slowly and not-so-surely? His body language suggests interest, and you can encourage him to close the distance in a variety of ways:

Five Lessons for Turkey Study

1. **Turkeys alarm putt:** Any member of the flock will do this, and it means you've been busted, buddy. If the gobbler you want is in range, steady yourself, and shoot it. If not, make that alibi.

2. **Turkeys move toward you:** Call and they will come—if they're so inclined. If you're confident that you've been undetected and that gobbling birds are interested, don't overdo it.

3. **Turkeys favor certain areas:** If you have seen birds repeatedly in a particular habitat, settle in for the long haul. Call sporadically. Punch the hunting clock, and be there when that gobbler slips in.

4. **Turkeys can be spooked:** If every bird that was ever spooked stayed that way, we would never get one. Try not to alarm them the next time, but resolve that you'll get a second chance. It may even be sooner rather than later.

5. **Turkeys don't commit to your calls:** Gobblers will sometimes drift away, and return. If their body language says they aren't primed to respond to your calls on your watch, realize they're on turkey time. Hunt on their watch, and give yourself enough time to do it seriously.

- Go to him if terrain provides cover, but don't stalk him. Stake a decoy out there to offer him visual evidence.
- You can make a lost hen call. Typically an autumn tactic for same-sex birds in broodless flocks, this technique works in spring for another reason—to arouse a male gobbler's interest. Loud friction calls and triple-reed diaphragms are great for this tactic.
- You can use a box call to crank up the volume, and cutt dramatically at the bird. What it sounds like on the gobbler's end of things is anyone's guess, but clearly this strategy can pull birds in from far away.

Body Language—Silent but Deadly

He's coming, you can just feel it, but he's not really letting you know that. Your sixth sense says, "Stay ready."

Spring gobblers will often close ground after your initial calls, but may stay silent. Always listen hard for steps in the leaves (first assuming it might be another hunter), and for spitting and drumming, which are kinds of calls—or at least auditory features—that hens listen for as strutting gobblers approach.

Sometimes, too, it pays for you to be quiet when dealing with a silent bird. Have confidence he may be coming, and sometimes he will be. Good camouflage options will help you stay hidden. A blind will hide you completely. Don't rule out that a hen may have intercepted him too.

Pay attention to how a gobbler acts when alone, and with other turkeys. If hens and jakes are approaching your setup, the dominant bird will often be the last to come in, delayed by his slowly strutting form. Wait. Watch. It's important to get your shotgun up, and freeze as the female birds, juvenile males, and subdominant toms pass in range. Keep your eyes front, focusing on that strutting longbeard, and drop him. If a hen or jake busts you, sit tight. Sometimes the gobbler is so intent on breeding, he'll be oblivious—especially if those other turkeys come in way ahead of him.

If a big flock of turkeys gets together and moves away from

That gobbler is coming, you can just feel it. Your sixth sense says stay ready. Mike Jordan took this fine Texas Rio Grande gobbler under similar circumstances when he and the author returned to an area where they'd located turkeys that morning. Cold calling brought this silent longbeard in.

If everything fails to turn a gobbler your way, you can talk turkey-hunting strategy and calling tactics with buddies back at camp before the next hunt.

your setup and initial calling efforts, sit tight, and let things settle down. Often a few stragglers—especially subdominant two-year-olds—will be primed for answering your calls, and in some cases, they'll strut right to your position. Be ready.

If that tom comes, but sees fit to hide behind cover until you present visual evidence, wait him out. If he drifts, cluck. He may steer in just close enough to close the deal.

9

Odds Toward Ends

Plunk your seat cushion down in the wrong place, and your turkey hunt is over from the start.

Where you set up can make all the difference. You've got to envision what that roosted tom will do when he flies down. You've got to pick a place he'll come when you call him. When you choose where to set up, you need to consider shooting lanes, comfort zones, and anything that will make your sitting time more comfortable .

Wild turkeys have the advantage over human callers. The following ten scenarios describe common calling locations where reading the terrain and positioning yourself correctly can help increase odds of tagging that tough spring gobbler.

TEN CALLING SETUPS

1. Pasture Strut-Zone Setup: The trick here is to find the high point in the field, and set up nearby. After morning fly-down, gobblers sometimes prefer to enter pastures at their highest point. They often strut there,

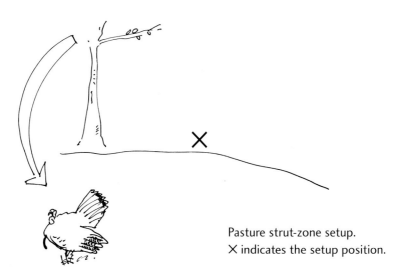

Pasture strut-zone setup.
X indicates the setup position.

trying to attract hens. Your morning setup before fly-down time should be between the roost and high point strut zone, but still inside concealing edge cover with shooting lanes in front of you. Cluck and softly yelp in position.

Hunter's Tip: Shooting lanes should provide open areas you can call a gobbler to, and where a clean head and neck shot is possible when a bird appears in range. When you set up, study the area in front of you. Find a balance of concealing cover and open spots. Carry small pruning shears to cut lanes (if the law allows), and make that setup shooter-friendly.

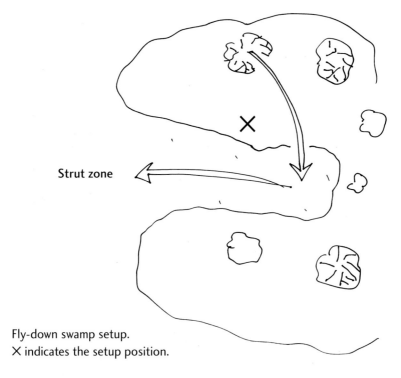

Strut zone

Fly-down swamp setup.
X indicates the setup position.

2. Fly-Down Swamp Setup: Find the dry ground. Swamp gobblers such as Osceolas and sometimes Easterns roost above water, which offers them a sense of security from predators below. They fly down to dry areas inside that swamp and move to open fields. Establish your setup somewhere along the dry-land travel lane between swamp roosting areas and strut zones. Tree call to turkeys on the roost, then wait.

Hunter's Tip: If you've patterned these swamp turkeys, use a hub-style camouflage blind along that dry travel lane between the swamp roost and strut zone.

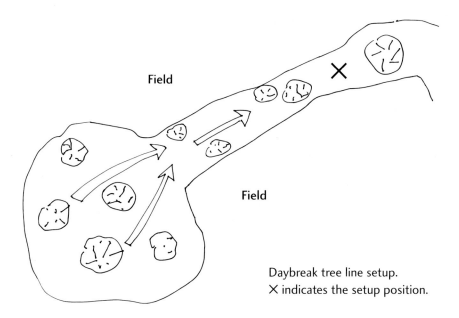

Daybreak tree line setup.
X indicates the setup position.

3. Daybreak Tree Line Setup: You've got to find what I like to refer to as "the landing strip" to make this calling setup. Some gobblers roost in wooded cover and fly down into forested lanes between fields as they move. Texas Rios, challenged by sparse cover, prefer this concealed mode of travel. You hear their gobbles but they sometimes move along to strut zones without being seen. Place your setup inside that tree line, along their fly-down landing strip. Look for snakes, prickly pear cacti, and uncomfortable sitting arrangements with your penlight in the pre-dawn hours. Turkey movement along this travel lane should allow you to call to birds as they ease along these tree line spots. If the vocal turkeys are at some distance, call more emphatically. If closing, soften it up. Sometimes gobblers will break away from concealed cover and move across adjacent open fields to your setup. Be ready.

Hunter's Tip: Roosted turkeys don't always move in predictable ways. They may fly directly into fields. They may move away through thick cover in the other direction. Scouting to pattern birds ahead of time can help predict fly-down probability. Locate gobblers the night before, and slip inside that tree line early the next morning. Once they're on the ground—especially if you've set up within 100 yards of birds—a hands-free diaphragm helps you lure these landing-strip turkeys into range.

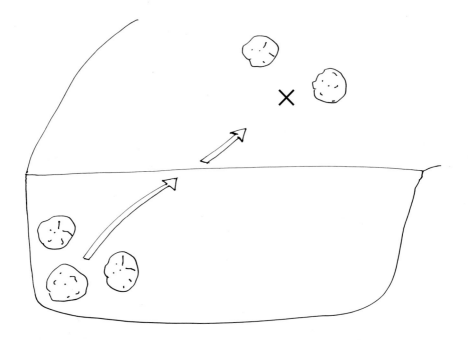

Sunrise ridgetop setup. ✕ indicates the setup position.

4. Sunrise Ridgetop Setup: For this one, you've got to rise above the turkeys and call them up to you. If the birds are roosted on the hillside, and you've used locator calls the evening before to pinpoint them, this setup is for you. Put yourself on the plateau above them before fly-down time. Initiate a conversation while they're on the roost (by tree calling), or just after fly-down (clucks and yelping), or both. If those birds happened to fly to their roost from your position the night before, they may fly right back down there again—with you in position. It may take some time, and turkeys may not move until midmorning, but sometimes that early rise is worth it.

Hunter's Tip: If you've tried this setup approach, and gobblers have stayed with hens after fly-down, sneak back in there later in the day after hunting elsewhere. Use a crow call to locate potential gobblers, and if none respond, slip back into position. Sometimes a roaming tom will answer to turkey calling immediately, and walk up that hillside to your plateau setup. In states where afternoon hunting is permitted, you can be there before fly-up time to intercept turkeys before they go to roost on that hillside, especially if it's a regular haunt for the birds.

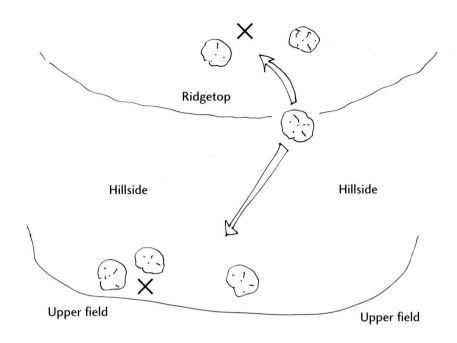

Sloping hillside setup. X indicates the setup positions.

5. Sloping Hillside Setup: Say you've patterned a particular gobbler or group of turkeys enough that you know they prefer to fly down to one of two spots in the morning—on opposite sides of the ridge. Two setups are required, but you need to choose just one. They may roost on the steep hillside, and fly down to the ridge-top flat. They may roost on that hillside, and sail down to the upper field zone. Flip a coin. Your odds here are 50-50. To increase your chances, put a buddy at one setup, while you take the other. Sit tight, call sporadically, and for safety's sake, agree on a specific meeting place. Never move on each other. It's a good plan, and you can communicate by walkie-talkie where legal. If the plan fails, use crow calls or some other locator call/signal to let the your partner know you're coming to meet him.

Hunter's Tip: If you're going out alone, try to roost these birds the night before your hunt. Watch where they fly up from to their roost trees. That's exactly where you want to be the next morning. Forget about the other option for now. Set your alarm clock an hour earlier, and hike back to that location well before sunrise. Sometimes those turkeys will fly-hop right down in front of you. If you call at all in this tight setup, make it a hands-free diaphragm. At this close range, turkeys will see you move if you use a box or pot-and-peg call.

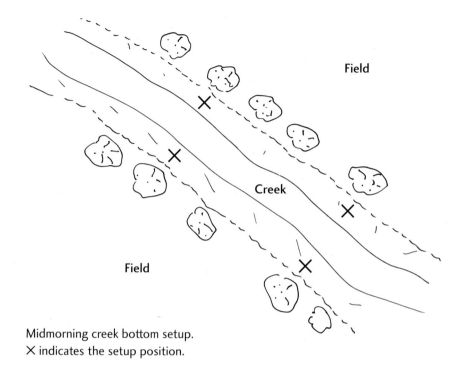

Midmorning creek bottom setup.
X indicates the setup position.

6. Midmorning Creek Bottom Setup: In this midmorning to midafternoon (where legal) situation, your setup may not be fixed. You may have to reposition. You might hear male birds respond to your turkey calls. You might see them strutting in open fields. The trick is to move slowly along creek banks, hidden by the terrain, using a crow call to locate nearby spring gobblers. Set up if you raise a bird. Use binoculars to view the areas ahead of you to avoid bumping turkeys, and perhaps to spy full-fan strutters in fields. Establish your setup on either side of the creek in the wooded tree line, and call that gobbler to your position. Try to get as close to the bird as you can. To avoid detection, belly-crawl a short distance to stake a decoy or two before calling. This creek-bottom technique is particularly effective in Midwestern states like Missouri and Iowa where farmland terrain affords this strategy.

Hunter's Tip: Many spring turkey hunters are familiar with the post-fly-down lull. It's the time gobblers are strutting and breeding with hens. As I was writing this book, I watched a video of a spring longbeard strutting for not one, but two, hens. In succession, he bred one female turkey, then the other. During this time he strutted but did not gobble. This visual example of the lull said it all. Since male birds aren't vocalizing during

In this midmorning to mid-afternoon (where legal) situation, the setup location is fluid. It involves locating spring gobblers, setting up on them, and maybe even repositioning. The trick is to move slowly along creek banks hidden by the terrain, using a crow, air-activated, or friction call to locate nearby spring gobblers at first, and setting up if you raise a bird.

Use binoculars to glass the areas ahead of you to avoid bumping turkeys, and possibly to spy full-fan strutters in fields.

this breeding activity, consider coursing along creek bottoms to find toms that are alone. Put your hunting speed on slow-pace cruise control. Check out the land you're covering piece by piece. The turkeys are there, somewhere.

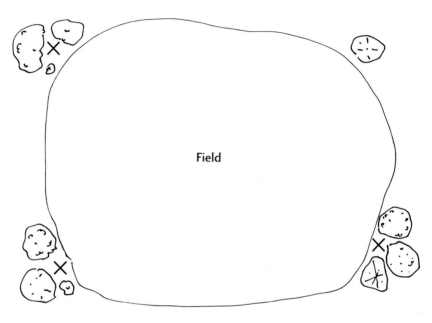

Midmorning sparse-cover setup. X indicates the setup positions.

7. Midmorning Sparse-Cover Setup: Turkeys are in the fields, but you don't know exactly where. Use sparse cover to establish setups in a general area where gobblers strut for hens. Sneak between wooded spots slowly and surely, using terrain to hide your movements. Set up and cold call to interest nearby birds on the chance of pulling them into your setup position. Merriams and Rios in open-area habitats often respond to this approach.

Hunter's Tip: Remember that game of hide-and-seek you played as a kid? Use that same sneaky approach as you move from one section of cover to another. Sometimes this strategy will put you inside a gobbler's comfort zone where he'll finally come to your calling.

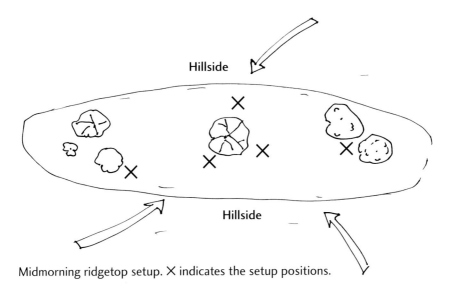

Hillside

Hillside

Midmorning ridgetop setup. ✕ indicates the setup positions.

8. Midmorning Ridgetop Setup: You could also call this one "Trolling for Gobblers." Ease along ridgetops during the morning lull. Use locator calls such as crow caws to raise spring gobblers that might be cruising for hens along hillside ridgetops. When you strike a vocal tom, set up so it will appear in shotgun or bow range. Plunk a decoy down there to hold the bird's attention.

Use locator calls such as crow cawing to raise spring gobblers that might be cruising along hillside ridgetops for hens. When you strike a vocal tom, set up so that bird will appear in shotgun or bow range as it comes to your calling on the lip of the hill. NATIONAL WILD TURKEY FEDERATION

Hunter's Tip: It's midmorning, and it's been a long time since you rolled out of your camp bunk. Find a broad-tree backrest, brush away leaves under your seat cushion and legs, and take a nap. The rest will refresh you for the second half of the morning's hunt.

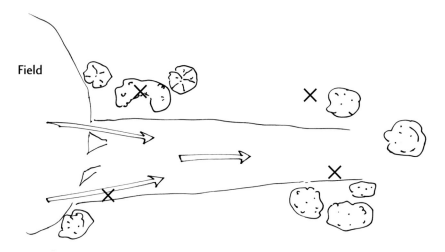

Afternoon transition zone setup. ✕ indicates the setup positions.

9. Afternoon Transition Zone Setup: Sometimes you have to intercept that gobbler. On afternoon hunts, where all-day opportunities are offered, set up in a natural funnel, bottleneck, or so-called "pinch point" between open-field strut zones and roost areas. Wild turkeys will often transition from open fields to edge cover, then to wooded areas during the late afternoon. Put yourself nearby and spark a gobbler's interest by cold calling. Set up near open lanes, game trails, and creek bottoms.

Hunter's Tip: Mix and match decoy configurations. Place a hen fake with a jake. Stake out several jakes and no hens. Call often to draw in nearby turkeys for a look. Sometimes they seem to come just out of curiosity.

Mix and match turkey decoy configurations. Use a single lone hen. Put a hen fake with a jake. Stake out several jakes and no hens. Use a full fan strutter, jake, and several hens. MOSSY OAK/NATIONAL WILD TURKEY FEDERATION

Did you hunt roosted birds that morning, and have them walk off after fly-down? In states where afternoon spring gobbler hunting is legal, return to the exact location. Wait for turkeys to go their roost, and pick out a strutter as it steps along the travel zone. You might not even need to call. NATIONAL WILD TURKEY FEDERATION

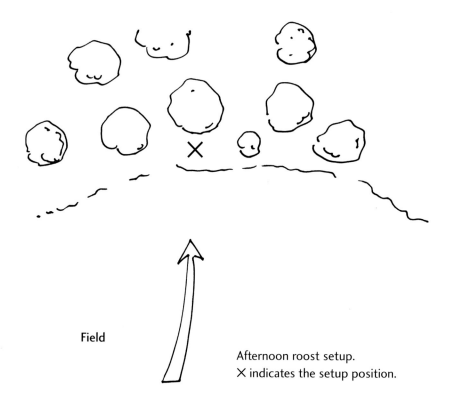

Field

Afternoon roost setup.
✕ indicates the setup position.

10. Afternoon Roost Setup: You're back where you started that morning. Position yourself close to the roost, concealed by edge cover, before
turkeys leave the fields to fly up into trees. If you know the birds and
their patterns, and you know which direction they'll come from and
where they'll likely go, sit tight. If not, locate turkeys somewhere along
this travel zone and position yourself to call a gobbler in. This is similar to
the morning setup before fly-down, but reversed. The turkeys are now
going to roost. Be there.

Hunter's Tip: Did you hunt roosted birds in the morning, only to have
them walk off after fly-down? In states where afternoon spring gobbler
hunting is legal, you can return to the exact location. Wait for turkeys to
go to their roost, and pick out a strutter as he steps along that travel zone.
You might not even need to call.

AUTUMN AND WINTER FLOCK CALLING CHALLENGES

The full range of fall and winter turkey hunting tactics is covered in my book, *Fall and Winter Turkey Hunter's Handbook* (Stackpole Books, 2007). I encourage all of you turkey hunters and callers to add it to your personal library. In the meantime, here are some autumn and winter calling challenges, and how you might respond.

Challenge No. 1: You've poorly scattered flocked-up autumn or winter turkeys, and they have flown into the trees above you.

Response: Flush this flock again by walking under them. Find a good setup somewhere in the center of the departed birds, and call when the turkeys begin talking again.

Challenge No. 2: You've flushed a male-only group.

Response: Set up at that spot until you're convinced they've regrouped. Hunt that day. Hunt the next. They may return immedi-

John Byrne and son J. T. Byrne of Lowry, Virginia, took these two fall longbeards on a New York state hunt after first flushing the all-gobbler flock with dogs, then calling the turkeys back to the break site.

ately, despite what you've read and heard elsewhere. You might begin calling by making three coarse gobbler yelps. If you need to make a *kee-kee-run*, do that.

Challenge No. 3: You've seen and heard a gobbler flock fighting to establish pecking order after fly-down.

Response: Set up there early the next morning. At fly-down, call with fighting purrs, agitated clucks, yelps, and even gobbles. Have that gun on your knee or bow at your side for the moment that first red head periscopes into range.

A facemask is essential in most turkey calling setup situations. It gives the hunter and caller confidence.

Challenge No. 4: You know where the fall or winter flock roosts, and where it feeds.

Response: Set up early between the roost trees and the feeding zone. Either softly tree yelp right before or after the roosted birds begin calling, or remain quiet until the flock begins to assemble after fly-down time.

Challenge No. 5: A flockless individual turkey answers you in the woods while you cold call.

Response: Imitate whatever vocalization it makes. Match a cluck to a cluck, a gobbler yelp to a gobbler yelp, a *kee-kee* to a *kee-kee*. Don't get fancy. Imitate the solo bird.

Challenge No. 6: The family flock's brood hen begins to assembly yelp in an attempt to call young turkeys to that position.

Response: Stand and slowly walk toward the bird. Ideally, she'll run off and stop calling. Return to your setup, and resume calling, imitating the most vocal turkey in that family flock.

Challenge No. 7: A flock of turkeys is feeding toward you in a direct line as you slip undetected through the woods or fields.

Response: If you're standing close to the moving birds, lean against a concealing tree, your gun or bow ready. If the flock begins drifting off, you might be able to steer them in your direction with a soft cluck, yelp, *kee-kee*, or *kee-kee-run*, after identifying flock composition.

Challenge No. 8: You've drawn an arrow and let it fly, missing the bird.

Response: Sit tight. Slowly nock another arrow. A released arrow is obviously quieter than a gun blast. If you've fired a load of pellets, and whiffed, stay put. Be patient, even though frustration rises. Call content-

Kevin Evans and son Cody took this October New York state wild turkey by calling the bird in after morning fly-down.

edly after the miss to assure turkeys all is well. A gun blast will likely flush birds, which you can later call back in to your position—or after you reposition. Yes, turkeys will come back to the same general spot, even after the loud bark of a scattergun.

Challenge No. 9: You're bored with your setup.

Response: Work on your calling. Empty the contents of your vest. Tune calls. Turkey sounds can entice roving flocks or single birds. Some might come in silently, so stay alert.

You've drawn an arrow, and let it fly—and missed the turkey. Sit tight. Slowly nock another arrow. Be patient, despite your frustration. Call contentedly after the miss to assure turkeys all is well. You may get another shot.

LUKE FASOLDT/NATIONAL WILD TURKEY FEDERATION

Yes, turkeys will come back to the same general spot, even after the loud bark of a scattergun. It may take time, but . . .

NATIONAL WILD TURKEY FEDERATION

SHOULD YOU STAY OR SHOULD YOU GO?

You've roosted a gobbler on public land, gotten up early the next morning, and driven your truck to the two-track road in the hills that will put you within walking distance of that turkey. You've slunk in there silently, eased into your setup, and everything is in place. A half hour before daybreak, the turkey gobbles; you tree call back; all's well until you hear another caller slink in and sit down on the other side of that bird. You were certain you had the place and the gobbler to yourself. Now what do you do? Do you try to outcall the guy to bring the turkey to you? Do you confront the interloper, ruining the hunt for both of you? Do you slip back to your truck and find another gobbler to hunt?

Trying to outcall the other hunter could work, but it creates a competitive and possibly dangerous situation. You could try to hang in there until your competition leaves, or simply walk in the other direction to locate another gobbler. Going back to your truck, and driving off to find another fresh bird to call and hunt is likely the most reasonable move. You can always return to the original location later in the day, week, or season.

During my turkey-hunting seminars, hunters often raise similar questions. As public land opportunities decrease in some areas, resulting in too many hunters and too little land, such instances seem all too common. Solutions:

1. Gain permission to hunt on private land.
2. Buy land to hunt.
3. Hunt public land during weekdays, or later in the season.

Keeping a level head is the best move, even though you've invested plenty of effort finding a particular gobbler. Look at it this way: your hunting time is extended, and that isn't such a bad thing.

You've roosted a gobbler on public land, gotten up early the next morning. You've slunk in there perfectly. A half hour before daybreak, the turkey gobbles; you tree call back. All's well until you hear another caller slink in and sit down on the other side of that bird. You were certain you had the place and the gobbler to yourself. Now what do you do? NATIONAL WILD TURKEY FEDERATION

CLOSE THE CALLING DEAL

Your homework has paid off and a gobbler is coming to your calls. Don't fail the final exam. Knowing when to take the shot could be the most critical moment of the hunt.

A wild turkey steps into range. Scouting, locating, and calling have all paid off, but suddenly that black eye drills you. The bird flicks its wings, and turns. It's now or, in a second or two, never. Knowing when to pull the trigger is crucial. Here's how to close the deal.

Step off distances. If you are not operating under pressure from either a gobbling or approaching bird, step off the distances to landmarks near your setup before getting into position. Note the distances to clearings, hilltops, brushy cover, trees. Visualize the landmarks at the limit of your shooting range.

If possible, set up against a tree that is at least as wide as your shoulders and as high as your head. Make sure you have a clear view of the shooting range in front of you and to each side. Point your gun in the direction you last heard the turkey. When the bird appears, use the landmarks as a reference for the distance of the shot. Limit your movement and adjust your position only when the bird's head is obscured behind cover. Make the shot only when the bird is in range and when the bird's head and neck are completely exposed.

Use range-finding devices. Hand-held range finders can give precise yardage readings if you'd rather not take the time to measure distance with steps or don't trust your judgment of distances. Big game hunters and bowhunters use range finders routinely, and these devices work for turkey hunters too. Practice using the range finder before you turkey hunt though. You and a buddy can wager friendly bets on shooting distances, and learn as you go.

Use decoy sets. Waterfowlers habitually place decoys in gun range. Turkey hunters can do the same. Hen and jake decoys can be staked at 25 to 30 yards, though some hunters prefer to set them even closer. Tighter sets will draw strutters nearer sometimes. If your decoys are placed well in range of your gun or bow, you'll still have a shot if the turkey hangs up just beyond the decoys. Either step off the distance or use your range finder before staking the decoys.

Your homework has paid off and a gobbler is coming to your calls. Don't fail the final exam. Knowing when to take the shot could be the most critical moment of the hunt. NATIONAL WILD TURKEY FEDERATION

In spring, gobblers often address jake decoys directly. Face the jake slightly toward you so that when the tom squares off with the juvenile fake, his back will be to you. Keep your shoulder pointed toward the decoy. If the other gobbler thrashes the decoy, enjoy the show before touching off the shot.

Set your limits. After finding the effective range of your shotgun, don't fire at a bird beyond that distance. Many of my hunting buddies like to say, "Forty yards is the magic number." Some turkeys will only come so far, though. If a bird is at marginal range, let it drift away or try to lure him closer. The key is to be patient.

If you're pinned down, wait for a strutter to turn his fan toward you. Then point your gun. If a gobbler keeps strutting, cluck to get it to raise its head. Shoot after he extends it. Don't rush. Don't panic. Enjoy those final moments. A strutting longbeard is a powerful image. Savor it.

Okay, that turkey is coming to your calls. Make sure you have a clear view of your shooting range in front of you and to each side. Point your gun in the direction you last heard the turkey. When the bird appears, use the landmarks as a reference to determine the distance of the shot.

Tagging turkeys is fun—no doubt about it. But watching them respond to your calls is also sweet.

Rehearse the shot. Before a turkey ever approaches your setup, make a mental picture of when you'll shoot. Consider a variety of scenarios— the bird marching in from the left, sneaking in from the right, strutting in straight around the large oak in front of you. Remember: birds will often do something you didn't quite plan on. Be ready to adapt, and know where you can make your shots. By analogy, it's like a quarterback dropping back to pass and looking downfield for his receivers. As with football's passing game, there are often several options for closing the deal. Choose the best one.

You've called that spring gobbler in, and taken it with a sure shot. Don't forget to tag your bird during all the excitement.
NATIONAL WILD TURKEY FEDERATION

Other hunters may have heard you calling. Your vocalizations might be convincing enough that they think you're a real bird. They might also be interested in the gobbler you're calling. Be aware of the ongoing situation at all times.
NATIONAL WILD TURKEY FEDERATION

Identify your target. Don't shoot at mere turkey sounds, colors or movements. Identify physical characteristics of the bird: head, beard (expected on gobblers; much rarer on hens), breast feathers (black-tipped on gobblers; brown-tipped on hens), feet (gobblers usually have spurs; hens don't), etc. Wait until you identify the entire turkey, not just parts of the bird.

If you're using a shotgun, shoot only the head and neck when that legal turkey is in range. Body shots generally cripple wild turkeys. Wounding a wild turkey should be avoided by taking only reliable shots. Remember this too: other hunters may have heard you calling. Your vocalizations might be convincing enough to them that they think you're a real bird. They might also be interested in the gobbler you're calling. Be aware of the ongoing situation at all times.

Watch that birdy. When suspicious, turkeys will drill you with their hyper-paranoid stare. They'll flick their wing tips. They'll putt, pirouette, and stride away. Once you've been detected, the game is in its final seconds. If that turkey is out of range, let it go. If you have a clean shot, take it.

If you miss, sometimes calling will calm birds briefly before you can make another shot. I once missed a Texas gobbler at five

If wild turkeys you're hunting come to your calls but move out of range, let them go. They may come closer as they search out the source of your vocalizations.

steps, and called enough after the miss to stall it and a traveling buddy at 47 yards. It's the longest shot I've ever taken by necessity. I made it with a sense of how the extended-range load would work. It did.

Know your firearm and load. Shoot your gun with various loads at comfortable distances—an exercise that should be an under-40-yard game, and 20 to 35 yards is even better. To know when to pull the trigger, pattern your shotgun using life-size head and neck turkey targets. Use the choke, load, and gun you'll tote on hunts. Shoot from various distances. Count concentrated target hits. Gain confidence in your firepower. It's one less thing to think about when that turkey answers your calls, and walks into range.

To know when to pull the trigger, pattern your shotgun using life-size head and neck turkey targets.

When pre-hunt patterning, use the choke, load, and gun you'll tote on hunts.

Try out different turkey choke tubes with your shotgun and load to see which one offers the best pattern density.

Trust your guide. If you hunt with professional turkey guides, trust their judgment when they call the shot—within reason, of course. These folks deal with a variety of hunters, from the absolutely inexperienced to the veteran gunner. In the end though, you pull the trigger, and you tag the bird.

If you can, meet the guide before going afield, and discuss your preferences for the hunt. Listen to them too. Ideally your hunting guide should know your gun's limitations, the ammo you're using, and your experience level. If you feel uncomfortable taking shots at longer distances, tell the guide. It's your hunt, after all. On the other hand, if you're confident taking a shot and the guide questions it, consider his or her advice. Some places conduct pre-hunt lodge discussions the night before clients and guides go afield. If the turkey camp you're visiting doesn't allow time for hunters and guides to get familiar with each other, suggest it.

Let it flow. As the turkey approaches, move the muzzle of your gun with imperceptible ease, but stay trained on the turkey's head. Anticipate when you'll make the shot based on your guess as to what the turkey will do. When it steps into range, take a second to concentrate, then shoot.

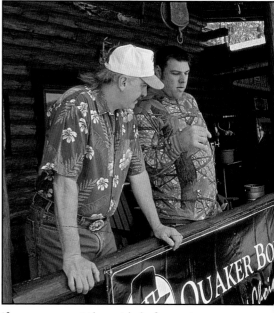

If you can, meet the guide before going afield, and discuss your preferences for the hunt.

Often a gobbler will strut in a shooting lane, if only to do his thing in full view of the hen you're imitating. Your gun barrel should point in that direction and drift slowly with his movements as the gobbler passes behind trees blocking his wary view from you.

Relax—but not too much. Both turkey fever and nonchalance will make you miss. Bear down in the moment of truth, and squeeze off the shot. Understanding when to pull the trigger is a big, but often overlooked, part of the equation. Using all your turkey calling abilities, you should be able to close the deal.

WINGING IT

You've called that strutting gobbler into range, aimed at his fist-sized noggin, and fired. Problem is, he flopped and got up like a boxer in the ring with some fight left in him. It's your move: now or never. That knockout punch you threw failed to deliver.

You've tried calling a wild turkey into range, and squeezing off a shot aimed at the standing bird's head and neck. You've failed. Though it's not the best way to anchor a spring gobbler, there are situations when taking a turkey on the wing is the only option, especially after missed chances— or worse yet, when the bird is wounded.

Shooting flying turkeys is almost always a Plan B option. Still there are ways to do it right:

- Speed rules. When a gobbler flushes, you've got just seconds to deliver the payload. Shoulder the shotgun smoothly but swiftly, stock to cheek. Keep your head down. Track that big bird, find the neck and head in your sight picture—better yet, its wild black eye—and hit that intended target with a steady action.

- Point it out. Right-handed wingshooters often hold their left index finger along the shotgun's forend to point at the target as they shoulder the firearm. (Southpaws reverse this.) Practice this when shooting sporting clays or other flying upland birds, and you'll be ready when the moment presents itself while turkey hunting.

- Shooting positions. Chances are you're sitting if you've called a gobbler into range. As it flushes, maneuver your body for stability the best you can. If the crippled bird is laboring off, stand up, then drop it. If you are standing, shoot that flushing turkey as you might other upland birds, but avoid body shots.

- React, don't think. Mount the shotgun. Find the target. Pull the trigger. Now tag that gobbler.

ARCHERY END GAME

You're confident that you can call that longbeard in—likely with a hands-free mouth diaphragm—before the moment of truth when you finally release the arrow.

Let's assume you spend so much time with your bow that you refer to that tool of turkey demise as "good buddy." Let's

Anticipate when you'll make the shot based on your guess as to what the turkey will do. Often a spring gobbler will strut in a shooting lane if only to do his thing in full view of the hen you're imitating. Your gun barrel should point in that direction, and drift slowly with his movements as the gobbler passes behind trees that block his wary view of you.

Mount the shotgun. Find the target. Pull the trigger. Now tag that gobbler.
NATIONAL WILD TURKEY FEDERATION

also take for granted you've scouted for spring gobblers. You know where that big boy you want roosts. You know where his hens like to sleep on limbs. You've sat and listened to them fly down, gather together, and move to nearby fields in the morning. You've seen that beast with the 10-inch beard strut his full fan. You're ready for game time.

Here are some proven ways to get that spring gobbler in arrowing range. The rest is up to you—oh yeah, and your good buddy.

Get that spring strutter close—real close. You can plot his demise by watching and patterning turkeys on a regular basis. It's really the only way to get inside that killing zone. Read the terrain. Is there a game trail that the longbeard likes to take to a strutting zone? Watch how sometimes turkeys like to enter an open spot (where hens can see them strut their wares) via the highest point on that expanse. Be there the next time.

How can an archer get close to that gobbler the next time he strolls into a field? Use a manmade blind constructed from natural materials to conceal your movements (though it limits mobility), or hunt with a model that's easy to transport and assemble. Or you can hunt turkeys on foot and call them to your position, drawing that bow when the strutter turns away or ducks behind a broad tree trunk.

It's a great feeling to be so comfortable with your bow that drawing it is as easy as riding a bike. To hit where you want, you must practice using

3-D turkey targets on a regular basis. One trick to gain confidence is to hunt fall squirrels with your bow, as a bushytail is roughly the size of a gobbler's neck and head. Much of the game is mental, and if you factor in solid mechanics, you'll kill turkeys.

Once you've patterned birds, and have a good idea where they'll be, stake turkey decoys at your effective bow range to fix a spring gobbler's strutting position. While some run-and-gun hunters may never tote decoys, the archer looking for solid arrow placement often relies on them. It's safe to say that the outdoor industry has never provided more turkey decoy options.

Packing a punch at the business end of your arrow is standard fare for the gobbler-chasing archer. Choose turkey-specific mechanical broadheads for solid flight and serious cutting diameter. Big-game broadheads work fine too.

When the moment of truth comes, time your shot on a calm, standing turkey in range with a sure draw and arrow release. That's the beauty of hunting spring gobblers. They strut and turn with predictable moves. Study that bird, then aim for that single feather on the wing butt, at the bottom of the fan, or in the head or base of the neck. After anchoring a turkey, put down your bow and quickly approach and step on the flopping bird's head or neck before removing the arrow (if it hasn't passed through).

Before the hunt, get a feel for the action of drawing on a turkey. Do so in your hunting clothes if possible. Practice arrowing targets from a hunting stool, a standing position, or on your backside to reflect live conditions. Always wear reliable, comfortable camouflage to instill confidence and concealment in your game plan.

Hunt archery-only seasons to extend your opportunities, and for the intangible pleasures such outings offer during both the spring and fall turkey seasons.

Don't stress too much over missed shots either, as it's part of the archery turkey experience. Sometimes strutting spring gobblers will simply move aside of the annoying stick that flew their way and missed, and you'll get another chance. Take it when it comes.

Postscript:
Last Hunter Standing

L
ike last at bats in baseball, you could hit a home run and win the game, or strike out and be the goat. Like last call at the local sports bar, you know you should just go home and get some sleep, but you don't. You're out there again chasing spring gobblers.

You've been at it since March where you started down south in some state like Florida or Georgia. Now you're putting the season to bed in late May. Other guys are bass fishing. You set your alarm for earlier times each ensuing week. You're the last man standing in the turkey woods.

You've lost 10 pounds since you first started a dozen weeks ago. It's a diet you won't ever hear mentioned on the network news.

You now sleep on the couch in the basement, ready to slip out well before dawn to sneak in on that roosted gobbler who's heard every call you've tried on him.

A turkey vest that was once loaded with a dozen extra calls, spare gloves, second facemask, and Global Positioning System, plus the state hunting regulations, is now down to half the weight.

You're only bringing a couple calls along these days. You wear your facemask around your neck, ready to pull it up at that first

You stay there a long time just thinking the whole thing over. Then with a war whoop or two, it hits you: you pump your fist in the air like a guy who has won a game in the bottom of the ninth. You talked to a turkey one more time in its language, and fooled that wild bird into range. Calling matters.

A hilltop gobbler will get a turkey caller's attention. NATIONAL WILD TURKEY FEDERATION

setup. You know the place you're hunting so well that a GPS isn't necessary anymore. You know the lawbook by heart. You've passed on legal jakes. You've come close to killing that big tom you want two times, just missing on both hunts. On the first encounter the longbeard hung back and let the shortbeard cruise in to check things out.

The second time, the jake and the adult gobbler swung in real close, but behind you. No dice. Afterward, you clicked your shotgun safety back on, and it almost sounded like the spitting part before the gobbler's drumming, and you got a quick scary buzz of adrenalin thinking it was that bird strutting in your lap. It wasn't.

You can still hear that longbeard's spitting and drumming like tinnitus after a rock concert. You need sleep. "When I'm dead," you mutter to yourself.

The third time, you throw the turkey-clinic book at him. When he double-gobbles at your yelps, you stay quiet—a long time. When he hammers back wondering where you are, you switch calls.

To emphasize you're the new hen in town, you yelp, walk away from that spot, set up, call one more time, shut up. He doesn't answer. You don't either. It's a long time before anything happens.

It's the last day of the season and you've had a good one. A missed shot down south, a handful of longbeards around the country, and now this: footsteps in the leaves coming from your right. It's not a squirrel . . .

it's the jake. Shortbeard comes in looking things over. The jake moves on past, and you catch a glimpse of black coming in, popping into strut. He gobbles hard.

Long sweet seconds pass. He's in range. You cluck. The longbeard and jake both lift their heads. After you pull the trigger, you give thanks. You stay there a long time just thinking the whole thing over. Then with a war whoop or two, it hits you: you pump your fist in the air like any guy who has won a game in the bottom of the ninth. The jake shock-gobbles far off, and you laugh. You talked to a turkey one more time in its language, and fooled that wild bird into range. Calling matters.

Appendix

Turkey-calling contests judged by human ears are one thing. Vocalizations regarded by real turkeys in a hunting situation are yet another. NATIONAL WILD TURKEY FEDERATION

COMPETITION CALLING

Turkey-calling contests judged by human ears are one thing. Vocalizations regarded by real turkeys in a hunting situation are something different. True, many of the top callers earned their reputations both on the convention stage and in the turkey woods. Then again, just because you'll never hoist a trophy at such an event doesn't mean you can't learn to talk turkey in the woods—and shoulder the ultimate prize. Even some real hens and gobblers would fail to make the first-round cut in a calling contest.

To call effectively in both a hunting situation and on the calling stage you need to master many aspects of turkey calling:

- Know the proper number of notes in a particular vocalization.
- Space the notes properly.
- Render the exact length of each note for particular calls.
- Offer the right volume for each vocalization.
- Replicate the correct pitch of each call.
- Recognize calling rhythm to convince human judges (and real birds).

CALLMAKING CONTACTS AND CALLING RESOURCES

Cane Creek Calls: Offers handcrafted slate, glass, aluminum, and box friction calls. Owner Doug Adkins's "Pro Custom Series" calls are made with African mahogany matched with a hickory striker.
Location: 60 Jasmine Drive, Jenkins, KY 41537.
Contact: 606-832-2243; www.canecreekcalls.com.

Cody Turkey Calls: Bill Zearing's Cody slate and glass wood pots come with hickory strikers. The handmade 6.5 Cody One Sider box call offers a Concaved Lid/Vertical Core construction.
Location: 65A Danner Road, Halifax, PA 17032.
Contact: 717-362-8413; www.codyturkeycalls.com.

D. Marlin Watkins: Watkins is a custom callmaker who tries to get as many turkeys into one box as he possibly can, including spring and fall vocalizations. Beautiful box calls with high-quality turkey-talk potential.
Location: P.O. Box 100, Summitville, OH 43962.
Contact: 330-223-2683; dwatkins@seseng.com.

Hunter's Specialties: David and Carman Forbes make glass, double glass, slate, brushed aluminum, and a variety of other calling surfaces on their pot-and-peg offerings. Strikers: Rosewood, acrylic, and carbon, among other materials. (The rosewood is a personal favorite, and works with a variety of pots.) Their Cutter Deuce Box call is waterproof/chalk-free.
Location: 6000 Huntington Ct. NE, Cedar Rapids, IA 52402.
Contact: 319-395-0321; www.hunterspec.com.

Hunter's Specialties® *Real Strut Talk* DVD features actual wild turkey vocalizations, and diaphragm calls. HUNTER'S SPECIALTIES®

Knight & Hale Game Calls: Knight & Hale's "Hammer" series offers four super friction calls with their new Sla-Tek surface: the Yella Hammer (for softer tree yelps, clucks, and purrs), Silver Hammer (aluminum for high-pitched calling on windy days), Slate Hammer (Pennsylvania slate), and Glass Hammer (for *kee-kees*, raspy hen yelps, and rowdy cutts and cackles). Knight & Hale Super Strikers are waterproof.
Contact: www.knightandhale.com/

Legacy Game Calls: William and Shannon Terry's "Trauma Series" friction calls have slate and crystal surfaces with bloodwood pots, and a so-called Sling Blade box (purpleheart lid/black walnut bottom), plus the "Bounty Hunter" series box call (purpleheart/mahogany), and pot-and-peg (glass/walnut or slate/glass). Hickory strikers.
Location: 2211 Ogden Rd., Rock Hill, SC 29730.
Contact: www.gameacc.net.

Pat dry, then store your mouth calls in a plastic case or bag in the refrigerator. This provides a cool, dark environment, which keeps reeds tight, providing optimum sound.

Lynch Worldwide: Mahogany and walnut box calls, including the classic World Champion. Pot and pegs: Pro Slate and Over & Under options.
Location: 1100 Smith Avenue, Thomasville, GA 31792.
Contact: 229-226-5793; www.lynchworldwide.com.

M.A.D. Calls: The "Heavy Metal" friction call doesn't play Metallica songs, but the aluminum pot is waterproof and projects far. Two strikers are included—a Rainy Day Carbon and Purpleheart wood peg. Other calls round out the options.
Contact: www.kolpin.com.

Midwest Turkey Call Supply: They don't make the calls, but they sell possibly the widest variety of turkey callmaker/call options available in one location.
Address: Midwest Turkey Call Supply, R.R. 3, Box 354D, Sullivan, IL 61951.
Contact: 800-541-1638; www.midwestturkeycall.com.

National Wild Turkey Federation: "Sounds of the Wild Turkey" at http://www.nwtf.org/nwtf_newsroom/turkey_calls.html.
Telephone number: (800)THE-NWTF.

Primos Hunting Calls: Will Primos offers a Wet Box and Power Crystal pot-and-peg, with Wet Weather striker. Other options include slate, glass, and aluminum. The well-known Heartbreaker is a purpleheart lid matched with a mahogany box. Fall hunters can opt for their Kee-Kee Striker.
Contact: www.primos.com.

Quaker Boy Game Calls: Dick and Chris Kirby's calls have been around for decades, including the Easy Yelper (push-pin), boat-paddle options, and their Hurricane waterproof no-chalk box. They sell pot/peg glass- and slate-faced calls, plus a variety of strikers. Triple Threat is a 3-in-1 pot with a slate, aluminum, and plexi surface.
Location: 5455 Webster Road, Orchard Park, NY 14127.
Contact: 1-800-544-1600; www.quakerboygamecalls.com.

Roberts Brothers Turkey Calls: Turkey hunters Tommy and Jerry Roberts are both cabinet makers and custom call producers. Craftsmanship is evident in these beautiful, functional pot-and-peg calls. Double-sided calling surfaces are glass-

fronted, and slate-backed. Strikers: all-weather aluminum or hardwood (both with surfacing stones).
Location: 3760 Old Oakwood Rd., Oakwood, GA 30566.
Contact: 770-536-7374; www.robertsbrothersturkeycalls.com.

Rut 'n' Strut Game Calls: Tim Sandford's pot calls include slate, glass, slate over glass, aluminum, copper over glass, and others. Woods vary, and include exotics. Strikers: flared tip/acorn balanced. Cedar long boxes, and scratch boxes.
Location: 11911 Ottawa Ave., Orlando, FL 32837.
Contact: 407-857-8397; rutnstrutgamecalls.com.

WoodHaven Custom Calls: Mike Pentecost's "The Cherry Classic Series" and "The Legend Series" provide pot-and-peg options (aluminum, crystal, glass, and slate). Strikers: laminated birch (flared tip), and oak. Boxes: walnut and cherry.
Location: P.O. Box 7, Heflin, AL 36264.
Contact: 256-463-5657; www.woodhavencustomcalls.com

Woods Wise: Jerry Peterson's Mystic box and pot-and-peg calls play wet (slate, glass, crystal, and synthetics).
Location: P.O. Box 681552 (W), Franklin, TN 37068.
Contact: 1-800-735-8182; www.woodswise.com.

Collection of box calls at Pete and Sherry Clare's Turkey Trot Acres.

RECOMMENDED READING

When not hunting and calling turkeys, you can read about hunting and calling—including the abbreviated list I share here. Read for pleasure, learning about particular calling strategies, experiences, and even technical information shared by others. Even seemingly unrelated material might help shape your sense of turkey calling history, vocalizations, and strategies. Here are some places to look:

Bland, Dwain. *Turkey Hunter's Digest*. Northbrook, IL: DBI Books, Inc., 1986. Bland reflects an enthusiasm for wild turkeys that involves fall, winter, and spring hunting, including calling strategies.

Casada, Jim. *America's Greatest Game Bird: Archibald Rutledge's Turkey-Hunting Tales*. Columbia: University of South Carolina Press, 1994. Edited and selected by Dr. Casada, this satisfying collection captures a bygone time period, and represents Archibald Rutledge's turkey writing. Rutledge's piece "Miss Seduction Struts Her Stuff," included here, details the effectiveness of one particular box call on a January 2, 1933, outing. If you want to know what it was like to hunt and call turkeys in the first half of the twentieth century, get your hands on this compilation.

Davis, Henry E. *The American Wild Turkey*. Georgetown, SC: Small-Arms Technical Publishing Company, 1949. An exact photographic reproduction of this vital work was reprinted in 1984 by Old Masters Publishers of Medon, Tennessee. Davis's work is a heavy dose of how-to writing, and is full of strategies that are still applicable today, while others seem antiquated in these modern times.

Dickson, James G. *The Wild Turkey: Biology & Management*. Mechanicsburg, PA: Stackpole Books, 1992. Edited by Dickson, there's no better collected text on wild turkey background, history, biology, habitat, and management through the early 1990s. Much of this scientific data is useful to the well-schooled turkey hunter and caller.

Harlan, Howard L. *Turkey Calls: An Enduring American Folk Art*. W. Crew Anderson, Editor-in-Chief. Harlan/Anderson Press, 1994. This book details the history of turkey calls, and includes images and drawings.

Henderson, David R. *The Ultimate Guide to Shotgunning*. Guilford, CT: The Lyons Press, 2003. This comprehensive guide on shotguns includes a chapter on turkey hunting that will help you close the deal after you call a turkey to your setup.

Hutto, Joe. *Illumination in the Flatwoods*. New York: The Lyons Press, 1995. No book better reflects an understanding of the wild turkey's flock behavior from egg to adulthood than this one. Here, naturalist Hutto establishes his human imprint on egg-incubated turkey poults, then records their relationships in journal-entry style.

Irmscher, Christoph. *John James Audubon: Writings & Drawings*. New York: The Library of America, 1999. Selected by Irmscher, Audubon's wild turkey writing presented here provides a historical glimpse into the nineteenth-century world of the wild turkey, including hunting strategies prevalent at the time.

McIlhenny, Edward A. *The Wild Turkey and Its Hunting*. Garden City, NY: Doubleday, Page & Company, 1914. As with the Davis book, Old Masters Publishers reprinted this title in 1984. While McIlhenny's name is installed as the author,

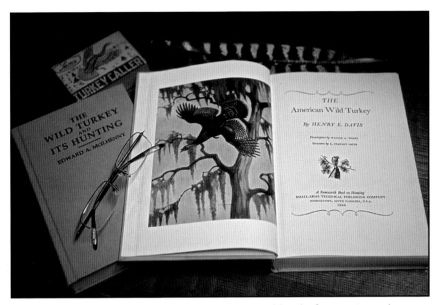

When not hunting and calling turkeys, you can read books for vicarious pleasure, learning about particular calling strategies, experiences, and even technical information shared by specific writers.

Charles L. Jordan (shot by a poacher in 1909) is responsible for much of the writing and all of the photographs included in this book. The chapters "On Callers and Calling" and "Calling Up the Lovelorn Gobbler" are must-reads for modern turkey calling enthusiasts.

Turkey Call. Various issues. Early 1970s-present. TC is the National Wild Turkey Federation's print magazine (six issues annually). Turkey calling is often featured in its pages.

Turkey & Turkey Hunting. Various issues. Early 1990s to present. Biologist Lovett E. Williams Jr. (he often details turkey vocalization insights), and editor-at-large Jim Casada (he commonly shares calling history and other subjects), among other writers, routinely contribute to this publication.

Williams, Lovett E., Jr. *Wild Turkey Country.* Gary Griffen, contributing photographer. Minocqua, WI: Willow Creek Press, 1991. Griffen's superb color images along with biologist Williams's text make this an instructive and enjoyable coffee table book, which illustrates the year-round life of the wild turkey.

You should also read, re-read, and carry with you, state hunting regulations wherever you chase and attempt to call wild turkeys. A routine online search for specific wildlife agencies will yield websites that provide more up-to-date information to help you plan your turkey hunts.

Wild turkeys are the best teachers of all. Spend time listening to these great game birds as often as possible, before, during, and after the season.

Glossary

alarm putt. One note of alarm per second. Uneven and unmistakable, this call tells the predator it has been spotted, and lets other turkeys know something is amiss.

assembly yelp. Of variable, even beats, this call can be half a dozen or more yelps. It is intended to call family flock members together.

beard. Grows from a gobbler's chest beginning at five months of age, and is found on some hens.

box call. A narrow, rectangular wooden turkey call with slightly arched sides and an attached paddle, also known as a lid.

cackle. An excited, uneven wild turkey call of half a dozen or more notes, often made when the bird flies off the roost. Length varies.

chalk. Rubbed on the underside of a box call paddle to improve the quality of turkey calling.

cluck. A plain cluck is one note. One- to three-note staccato wild turkey vocalizations of uneven beats can be used to begin a series of yelps.

cutt. A series of sharp, rapidly repeated clucks, often made to locate gobblers.

diaphragm call. Consists of one or more latex layers stretched across a horseshoe-shaped frame. It fits inside the roof of a caller's mouth. Short bursts of air blown across this call produce turkey vocalizations.

dressing calls. Preparing a turkey call for use. For box calls, this can mean chalking underneath the paddle. For pot-and-peg calls, it can involve rubbing a slate surface with sandpaper.

friction call. A turkey call requiring a caller to move one part of the call against another part to make vocalizations such as clucks and yelps.

gobble. Made by a male turkey to call a hen to its springtime position during the breeding season, as well as in the fall as gobblers contest pecking order.

jake. A male turkey under two years of age.

jenny. A female turkey under two years of age.

kee-kee. A three-note, uneven musical call made by young turkeys in the fall (and sometimes spring).

kee-kee-run. A four- to ten-note call made by young turkeys begun by the *kee-kee* and one yelp or more.

locator call. Any call which produces a sound that elicits a shock gobble from springtime male birds, or any turkey call that causes a silent turkey (male or female) to sound off.

longbeard. Term for an adult male turkey over two years of age. Beard lengths on this bird typically range from 7 to 10 inches, or more.

plain yelp. An even call of wide variation among hens (three to four per second), and gobblers (often three in succession).

purr. A soft call used to space turkeys while feeding, and a loud call (often called the fighting rattle) that is heard when turkeys contest pecking order.

push-pull call. A wooden box with a moveable plunger for making clucks, yelps, and purrs.

roost. The location where turkeys choose to sleep at night.

scratch box. Looks like a small box call without a paddle. The striker is moved across the box's lip.

setup. The location from which you choose to call, often at the base of a tree.

shock gobble. A seasonal springtime tendency for male turkeys to gobble to loud sounds, natural and unnatural.

spitting and drumming. The sound a strutting gobbler makes when strutting.

spur. The growth found on a male turkey's tarsus.

striker. The device used to create friction against the face of a pot-and-peg call or other friction call. Also called a peg. Many versions are used.

The wild turkey. NATIONAL WILD TURKEY FEDERATION

strutter. Term used to refer to a gobbler with its full fan displayed.

tree yelp. Soft and somewhat nasal in quality, this call is often the first heard in the morning. It consists of three to five notes made by a hen on the roost.

tube call. An open-ended cylinder with latex stretched across it and held in place. The caller blows air across that reed to produce turkey sounds.

vest. An article of turkey-hunting apparel that often includes pockets for calls, a game pouch, and a seat cushion.

wingbone call. A call made from the wing bones of a wild turkey, it can produce clucks and yelps in the right caller's hands.

Index